BEING LIGHT

Beyond the Veil of
The Golden Age

*A Light Server's Guide to Harnessing
the Energies of the New Earth*

GIA GOVINDA MARIE

BALBOA.
PRESS
A DIVISION OF HAY HOUSE

Balboa Press books may be ordered through booksellers or by contacting:

Balboa Press
A Division of Hay House
1663 Liberty Drive
Bloomington, IN 47403
www.balboapress.com
1 (877) 407-4847

Because of the dynamic nature of the Internet, any web addresses or
links contained in this book may have changed since publication and
may no longer be valid. The views expressed in this work are solely those
of the author and do not necessarily reflect the views of the publisher,
and the publisher hereby disclaims any responsibility for them.

The author of this book does not dispense medical advice or prescribe the use
of any technique as a form of treatment for physical, emotional, or medical
problems without the advice of a physician, either directly or indirectly. The
intent of the author is only to offer information of a general nature to help
you in your quest for emotional and spiritual well-being. In the event you use
any of the information in this book for yourself, which is your constitutional
right, the author and the publisher assume no responsibility for your actions.

Any people depicted in stock imagery provided by Thinkstock are
models, and such images are being used for illustrative purposes only.
Certain stock imagery © Thinkstock.

Print information available on the last page.

ISBN: 978-1-4525-9967-0 (sc)
ISBN: 978-1-4525-9968-7 (hc)
ISBN: 978-1-5043-2827-2 (e)

Library of Congress Control Number: 2015902996

Balboa Press rev. date: 03/30/2015

DEDICATION

To the beautiful seekers
of
light, truth, and greater eminence within.
May the compass of your heart guide you.

ACKNOWLEDGEMENTS

Eternal thanks to The Most Radiant One, the "Beings of Light", Aurora, my beloved Angels and Cosmic Guides, the Airborne Division of The Great White Brotherhood, Nature Spirits, and the Ascended Masters & Teachers that have graced me with their presence through the years and with the work on this project. To Blessed Mary for her endless demonstrations of love and healing. To my spiritual family and friends that have traveled this journey by my side as we continue to weave our tapestries on this plane ~ I love you all. And to Elfie, Alisa, and Kara for your everlasting love and encouragement in this endeavor.

Special thanks to Mother Nature for her unending support, education and nourishment in my life, as she has cradled me in her loving arms from the very beginning of my incarnation on this plane.

Loving acknowledgement to my beloved friend and rock connoisseur, Helen Sullivan, who crossed over during the creation of this book. Your insights, light, and laughter are with me always.

To Thorin, my ethereal White Knight, ever present, who now roams the meadows of Spirit.

Infinitely, eternally, forever, to my beautiful daughter Camille, who has enriched my life beyond measure.

WELCOME

Welcome to The Golden Age. We have entered an unprecedented time on the planet and throughout the Galaxies; a time of great truth, acceleration, activation and liberation. A time of self-remembrance at the deepest core level, and the long awaited reunion of beloved souls from long ago. The time has come, Dear Children of Light. We are in the NOW!

Within these pages you will find HOPE. You will find GUIDANCE. You will find GRACE, LOVE, and ANSWERS. I work with a group of divine Celestial Beings called the "Beings of Light". This higher dimensional group of Benevolent Beings consists of enlightened Angels, Ascended Masters, Elementals, Nature Spirits, and other beautiful Cosmic Guides. This Galactic Fleet of Light is associated with The Most Radiant One and can be described as the Airborne Division of The Great White Brotherhood*. Most recently, an additional advanced Being presented to assist me with my work on this project. This ethereal Cosmic Guide is named AURORA and is very honored to be of service to you, the planet, and humanity. It has been my tremendous honor and great privilege to work with these Radiant Beings and be a channel for their higher light frequency. I am truly humbled by the love and illumination they have showered upon me as we have worked side by side to raise the vibration of the planet.

The Beings of Light and Aurora are in full gratitude to those holding these pages and look forward to the new Era of Terra, as

---

* White referring to LIGHT

we merge more fully into The Golden Age of Light, co-creating the New Earth where there is perfect peace, love and harmony for ALL.

May you glow in inner illumination, as we stand UNITED AS ONE and serve the Kingdom of God in the new Heaven on Earth.

Infinite Love & Joy,
Gia

This book is presented in channeled format, and
has not been altered or edited in order to keep the
transmissions authentic and clear. As you bask in the
energy of these pages, may you feel a deep knowingness
and remembrance within your heart, as you raise your
vibrational frequency and begin your recalibration
process, journeying *beyond the veil* of The Golden Age.

Glory to God in the Highest
And Peace to the People on Earth...

Luke 2:14

WHO ARE
THE "BEINGS OF LIGHT"
AND AURORA

I AM Aurora. I serve on the Air Fleet of The Most Radiant One, beside the "Beings of Light". The "Beings of Light" encompass Archangels, The Great White Brotherhood, Christed ET's, Elementals, Cosmic Angels and Ascended Masters, a Sky Branch of The Great White Brotherhood, if you will. I have different assignments in different dimensions, working also with the I AM Presence and the violet flame teachings. I also guide the Star Fleet of The Most Radiant One, familiarly known to you as Master Jesus or "Sananda", and have taken a vow to assist in the most vital mission of assisting Planet Earth in its transition into a star.

As Aurora of Light, I come to bring you messages of PEACE, FAITH and LOVE. I work primarily from the 9th and 11th dimensions, at the right hand of The Most Radiant One, assisting all who wish to heal, transmute, and ascend. From our vantage point, we see the humans struggling to attain the light of consciousness, negating their circumstances through self-sabotage and fear. Have faith, Children of Light, for it is your Divine Destiny to walk hand-in-hand in the Light of Spirit, where ALL things are possible, as you most joyfully create the much anticipated and long-awaited Heaven on Earth, as your beautiful planet evolves beyond the veil of The Golden Age.

WHAT
IS
LIGHT BODY

Cosmic Nova:

The energetic matrix that surrounds the physical vessel as it prepares to shift into its perfected light body operates at an immense speed spinning, interacting and intertwining with the multidimensional layers of the Universe, radiating and rippling across all space and time... This multidimensional matrix houses the codes and keys to the entire Galaxy and Universe, and the power lies within YOU to activate and ignite the ancient memory of self. THE TIME IS NOW to awaken and tap into this infinite sea of knowledge, to at last merge with the Cosmic Pillar of Divine Light, to expand and reveal your true spiritual identity, your Divine Blueprint, your calling.

The cells and subatomic molecular structure of the human vessel hold the supreme intelligence of All That Is... As you nourish and fill your cells with light, you ignite the memory that is encapsulated throughout your Beingness. As you consciously work to build your Body of Light, you raise your frequency, allowing your soul to communicate with the cells in all living things around you. As you share your light with others, you increase the vibration of the planet; you become a precious link in the Great Shift.

Light is the most vital source on the planet and when you fill your vessel with LIGHT, you begin your activation process, restructuring, recalibrating, recoding your energetic matrix back to its original framework... You begin the process of shifting into your perfected LIGHT BODY.

Affirmation: I AM flooding my body with Christed Cosmic White Light now.

I AM living in my perfected light body now.

STREAMS OF LIGHT

Each new stream of energy saturating the earth plane raises the vibratory rate of humanity, preparing you for the Ascension process. As you bring more LIGHT into your body, you activate higher dimensional coding, reconnecting and reactivating your 12-strand DNA.

Streams of light shower the planet, adjusting and fine tuning the energies of All That Is in preparation for The Golden Age and beyond. As you merge with these energies and pull more light into your body, you oxygenate your nervous system, awakening ancient codes and keys within your soul, activating latent abilities that have laid dormant for decades, maybe even centuries, in your soul's blueprint. This is the time to awaken, to remember, to break down the barriers of illusion that have held you back from evolving into the highest aspect of your natural essence, your super-conscious state, your I AM Presence, to RADIATE. As you integrate these beams of light, you transform into your highest state of Being and your multidimensional soul emerges, accelerating your evolution. As you fill your body with light, you become a Transmitter of higher light energy. The vibratory frequency of humanity is raised, preparing mankind for its catapult into The Golden Age. I AM Aurora.

Affirmation: I AM integrating & assimilating the high vibrational frequencies showering the earth plane now.

I AM activating my dormant inner codings now.

THE
MAGIC OF NATURE

Nature holds the codes and keys to higher light knowledge. As you spend time in Nature, you respond to an inner coding, creating a high vibrational frequency that aligns you with your true remembrance of self and deeper understanding of All That Is.

The philharmonics of the body's energetic matrix are closely connected to nature's rhythm. As you cradle yourself in the arms of nature, you receive divine coding and downloads that support your mission and journey on this plane. As you embrace the crown glory of nature, a whole new tapestry presents, assisting you in resolving any questions or perplexities that may have eluded you for years, decades, or even lifetimes. As you forge the trail of higher consciousness, opening up to Mother Earth and communicating your intention for humanity and your soul's evolution, your path is lit, for nature holds the keys to the gateway of higher cosmic knowledge. As you bless and respect the Earth, you receive coded filaments, supporting your journey on this plane.

Dear Ones, we would ask that you live in harmony with nature, each and every day, for every species on the planet serves a purpose in the divine plan, mirroring back to you all you need to see, supplying you with guidance on your journey. We ask, have you ever really stopped to look at the beauty of nature and seen yourself in the Eyes of God? Have you ever listened to the sweet hum of spring peepers and cicadas, only to find yourself transported to a trance-like state, catapulted to what feels like a higher dimensional parallel reality...? This is because the essence of nature touches the deepest aspect of your original core blueprint, back to the beginning of time before your flame was separate from the Source. Mother Earth knows when you walk her sacred ground, she awaits your arrival and brings vital information to you through feelings, emotions, and creative insights and downloads. The flowers have messages for you, the birds, the bees, the trees and more. As you see the Spark of God in ALL living things, you awaken to the higher dimensional frequency of who you are and your soul emerges, shining light and awakening others. Accept Mother Earth's invitation to kick off your shoes, sit amongst the flowers and moss, walk the woods, meditate against a tree. Through your energetic connection with the earth, you set templates to anchor in higher light form. As you do so, you strengthen the Planetary Bridge and Crystalline Cosmic Grid, becoming a precious link in the Ascension process of the planet. Even your gentlest gesture of walking the earth and really *feeling* the grass on your bare feet is an act of merging with the Divine. Can you not feel the presence of God permeate every cell in your being through your state of centeredness, peace and calm, when you are in the arms of nature? This one-centeredness occurs as you merge with the splendid energy of the trees, the earth, the mountains, streams, meadows, and vast seas, for Mother Nature's aura is expansive and forms an elaborate matrix, encapsulating you in the sacredness of her womb. I AM Aurora.

Affirmation: I AM receiving now my Spirit-sanctioned infusions, downloads and mission directives.

I AM one with Nature and all of God's creatures.

BRINGERS OF LIGHT

You are a MAJESTIC Ray of Light... Release the illusional chains
that bind you and allow your magnificent spirit to SOAR.

How do we measure the concept of time...? What molecules
and subparticles bond together to place us exactly where we
are at any given time, including but not limited to, parallel
lives...? You chose to be here in this particular lifetime to hold
the frequency of Light, to expand your vision of Love, and
to assist as Guardians to usher this beautiful Planet Earth
into The Golden Age of Light. You wonder what your role
is, what your part in the Play is... We are here to tell you
that as you walk the Earth, you set energetic templates which
serve as portals to higher dimensional energy. In this way,
the waves of light that shower the Earth, as well as solar
flares, eclipses, and other energies associated with astrological
alignments can easily be anchored in and grounded. Those of
you reading these pages have come to serve as Ambassadors,
or Bringers of Light, if you will. Wherever you go, whatever
you do, you radiate your light and set energetic templates to
assist in transforming places on the planet. There may have
been times in your life when you wondered, "Where am I,
and what am I doing here"...? You may have taken what was
perceived to be a wrong turn, inadvertently gone around the
same block three or four times, or were drawn to travel to a
certain geographical location that may have left you feeling

daunted or perplexed. However, you were always guided and protected, for in your wanderings, you were not lost. Each of you reading these pages chose to come here at this particular time, to carry the frequency of LIGHT and to move more fully into the frequency of LOVE.

There are some of you who have wondered why you were placed in the particular earth families you are in. When you were younger, some of you may have experienced abuse or been extremely misunderstood by siblings or parents. You may look unlike any of your kin. And, though you were surrounded by many acquaintances growing up, you may have chosen to have just one or two close friends...confidantes, if you will. You were perhaps a loner and felt homesick for something that you couldn't quite place your finger on or assimilate. Some of you may have had traumatic experiences in your adult life which have led you to a deeper understanding and awakening. All of these circumstances, some tragic and treacherous as they may have been, served to evolve you into your highest potential. To search for the meaning of LIGHT and to bring Light to those around you, for you were placed exactly where you needed to be, to transform, heal and recalibrate the energy of others. To access the ability to understand, serve, and counsel other earthlings more fully, for you are Majestic Beings of Light placed on ASSIGNMENT on this plane. Tap into your soul's blueprint and remember the glorious gifts you came here to share with the world. I AM Aurora of Light and I bring you these messages today. I am here to assist you in awakening & honoring the I AM Presence within and to carry forth the violet flame of spiritual knowledge through remembrance of self and the eminence of light.

Affirmation: I AM a Bringer of Light here to assist humanity's healing and raise Conscious Awareness universally.

I AM Radiating love, peace and harmony to all Beings everywhere.

BODY OF LIGHT

As you evolve spiritually and drop density, you move into a higher vibrational body that enables you to explore other dimensional realities.

The multidimensional matrix that houses your physical body continues to evolve and prepare you for your emergence into the Light and acceleration into The Golden Age. As your light body upgrades and prepares, it vibrates into a spinning vortex which houses all the molecules and subparticles, containing the codes and keys to Nature and All That Is. As you bring more light into your body, you activate higher light frequencies, recoding, reconnecting and reactivating your DNA blueprint back to its original 12-strand state of being. As you fill your body with light, you help reinforce the Planetary Network of Light, and assist in the mass awakening of humanity.

Some have asked what will happen to electronics as the Golden Age continues to expand and emerge. Earthlings are caught up in the technological age of electronics and instant gratification, if you will. As Light Beings, you house your own inner "computer", so to speak and as you fully merge with the spherical energies of The Golden Age and evolve into the multidimensional being that you came here to be, you will be less interested in such "gadgets". Your body will be your electronic matrix. You will have everything you need within your Beingness, for you will be operating from your Heart Centers, which are infinitely multifaceted. You will be speaking with mental telepathy. You will be transporting yourself, teleporting, in your own personal craft, which is YOU. The demographics of the dark side have encouraged human beings to be distracted from nature, and has placed a candy store of electronics at your disposal to keep you separate from God, the Source, All That Is. We ask, have you ever allowed yourself to spend the day in nature and bask in the energies of the Divine which emanates from the trees, the ocean, the hills, the mountains, the rivers... For those of you who have, you know the feeling that permeates your consciousness. You feel the peace and Oneness, the calm, the centeredness. Nature was created by God to hold the codes and keys to the Awakening Soul, to nourish and heal you. So encourage your loved ones, your children, your kin, to go outside and spend time with the Elementals, for they are also the Guardians of the Earth and have much to teach you. Spend time communing with the great willow, the oak, the flowers, the velvety moss, for they contain vast information and knowledge waiting to be explored. Feel the tingling vibration of the light streaming through the trees as it speaks to you, for this is all part of your soul's education and evolution into the light.

The multi-crystalline structure of the human energy field contains millions of atoms and particles, vibrating at the speed of light, inviting you to merge with your light body. The technographics of the evolved light body allow you to explore other dimensional realities through astral travel and teleportation, for this is the way of the future in the New Era of Terra. Your body will be your "craft" and as you think of a desired geographical destination, you will be instantaneously transported there. This is possible, because as you transcend linear time, you raise your vibration and exist in a higher dimensional state of reality, which allows you to easily manifest your expansive vision and destination of choice. You will have the ability to travel through many portals of energy with magnificent colors, petals, tones and landscapes.

The goal on planet earth at this time is to fully realize your God Self, to become one with the I AM Presence, the spark of divinity in each and every one of you, to raise the vibration of humanity to a level of exalted spiritual comprehension, allowing you to merge with spherical time and space, to Ascend. As you fill your body with light, you build your frequency, preparing you for this flight. I AM Aurora.

Affirmation: I AM one with my Higher Self, my I AM Presence within.

I AM merging with my Light Body, integrating and assimilating All That I AM.

RAISE
YOUR FREQUENCY

When you evolve spiritually and raise your frequency, your light body SHIMMERS, emitting energy to all you meet.

As you embrace the waves of light enveloping the planet, you become a magnet for higher consciousness. Light, which is the energy of GOD, is the supreme intelligence of the Universe. When you fill your body with the Light, you raise your vibratory rate and emanate this magnificent frequency to all you meet. Stand or sit in stillness and state, "I AM filling my body with Christed Cosmic White Light now".

Light is the transmutational energy of God and as you fill your vessel with light each day, you build your Body of Light, allowing your multidimensional essence to emerge and grow. You become a precious link in the planet's Ascension process, raising the frequency of those around you, and strengthening the planetary grid. Where there is light, there can be no darkness, for the power of the LIGHT, or God, is all-encompassing. So White Light your vessels, Dear Ones. Allow your body to drink in the light. Every moment you think of it, fill your body with light. It can be as simple as "White Light, White Light, White Light". As you fill yourself with light, you become a BROADCASTER of higher dimensional frequency, drawing to you those souls and circumstances that can benefit from your energy, your light, your truth... Every person you come into contact with will be affected by your aura, raising the frequency of the planet, for when you live within the Universal Realm of Truth, a magnetic effect occurs, encouraging others to follow your example and live in a similar way. So White Light your loved ones, your family, your friends, your pets, the planet, for it will raise the vibration of all involved. I AM Aurora of Light and I come to serve you on this day.

Affirmation: I AM a magnet of higher consciousness.

I AM a Broadcaster of higher light frequency.

LOVE
IS THE ANSWER

The Light of your Heart is the GATEWAY through which your Higher Self communicates... As we traverse The Golden Age energies, humanity is required to embrace the uniqueness of ALL BEINGS, joining together in a unified Global cause.

If you could only know how much love there is for you in the higher realms of Spirit, you would never feel alone, for we are with you, softly whispering in your ear and enfolding you in our benevolent care of love, compassion and peace.

LOVE is the most powerful force in the Universe. It dissolves all separateness. In the days to come, humanity will be operating from their heart centers, much like we do in the Sky Borne Division of The Great White Brotherhood, beside The Most Radiant One, in the Galaxies of Spirit. When you speak with the voice of your heart, you allow the three-fold flame within the Secret Chamber of your Heart to blaze brightly, creating an energetic matrix that lights up the world, assisting with the planet's Ascension, Unity Consciousness, and Great Shift, into and beyond The Golden Age.

As human beings, you each have a basic soul purpose to LOVE. As you allow yourselves to Love and BE loved, you open up the Secret Chamber of your Heart, revealing your deeper personal mission and divine spiritual blueprint, for the Secret Chamber is the portal to higher light frequency. LOVE is the most precious gift in the Universe, and when you realize this, you activate a dormant 'password' well known throughout the cosmos...your matrix ignites and your life takes on new meaning. As you activate this portal of higher light knowledge, you place yourself in the direct flow of the Universal language of light, and your path is lit, for your heart is the seat of wisdom and connection to the Source through the subconscious mind. Through your heart, your questions shall be answered.

Love is the constant steady stream in the Universal tide of energy, and as you love yourself and others, you raise your energetic vibration, allowing your Higher Self to present and shine light on humanity. As you open up and merge with this I AM Presence, you activate this portal of higher dimensional knowledge within... You BECOME your Higher Self. Love your fellow Children of Light, even those not awakening at this time, for they too, have come to this plane for the opportunity to awaken to the Light of Spirit, to bask in the divine energy of Oneness, to evolve and transmute their earthborn frequency to a higher dimensional state of being so that they too, may Ascend in The Golden Age of Light. Everyone that you encounter on your journey came here with the initial intention of awakening and evolving into a higher dimensional being, and their presence around you is of no haphazard coincidence. For when you attain a certain level of consciousness, you release an electromagnetic pulse, attracting to you those souls that can benefit from your energy, your light, your truth.

LOVE transmutes all negative energy. We ask that you not waste time fighting over dogmatic or political issues, Dear Ones. It matters not what your religion of choice is, for when the Trinity of the *Great Creator* is formed with the *Intention* and *Good of All*, the Spark of Divinity is ignited in all mankind. Be kind and gracious to one another, all around the world, for where there is forgiveness, there is calm. Where there is peace, there is love. And where there is tolerance and equality allowing all people to be who they are, there is UNITY. The Seventh Golden Age is upon us, and we ask you to shower love on all of your planetary brothers and sisters, near and far, friend and foe, for this will assist Mother Earth tremendously in making her shift into the higher dimensional atmosphere. Fill your bodies with Love and Light, and radiate this amazing energy to the world each day. We bless and love you, and assist you greatly in strengthening the Bridge of Light. We are the "Beings of Light" and Aurora.

Affirmation: I AM welcoming the authenticity of souls around me, and joining hands in a Unified Global Mission.

I AM radiating love, peace and harmony to the World now.

THE
ASCENSION OF THE PLANET
IS GRADUAL

The process of Ascension is gradual. There is no "light switch" moment. You are not matter one day and LIGHT the next.

As we have previously stated, Dear Ones, the transition of your beautiful planet into a star is a gradual process and will take years to come into full fruition, for if everything were to happen all at once, you would simply combust!

Do not be stuck on timeframes, Beloveds, for we are operating in spherical time, unlike your linear time on earth. We do not have calendars, as you would say, we exist within matrixes of energy. The Ascension of your planet will take place gradually, so do not be slave to a specific day and time, lest you will be dismayed. For The Golden Age of Light does not happen in the blink of an eye, in the flip of a switch. It builds in layers and continues to evolve at a marked pace. You will know you have shifted into a higher reality as you step further through the veil in days and months to come. We ask that you stay the course, and live in truth, for TRUTH and LOVE are the most powerful sources to mankind. Love builds and strengthens the Crystalline Planetary Grid, or Christ Consciousness Grid, and Truth ignites the embers burning deep inside your original memory of Self, before you were separated from your flame of knowledge deep within. You will make the leap beyond the veil of The Golden

Age as you strengthen and repair the Bridge of Light. We honor and bless you on your most sacred journey always. I AM Aurora.

Affirmation: I AM a precious link in strengthening the Planetary Grid.

I AM vibrating in my highest frequency and truth in each and every moment.

THE
HEALING POWER OF
LIGHT

LIGHT is a living consciousness and responds instantaneously to your call...Build your Body of Light.

The power of light transforms any challenging situation. The more light you bring into your body, the higher the frequency. The higher the frequency, the closer you are to God, your Buddha Nature, All That Is.

LIGHT is a miraculous source of healing, and as you pull more light into your body, you oxygenate your nervous system accelerating your physical healing and soul's evolution. We ask you now to remember that you are Light Beings, and that any area of unease in the physical vessel can be healed with light. Call LIGHT to the areas of the body that are vying for your attention. Flood every single cell of your vessel with light and ask that the light be directed to any areas of pain or *dis-ease*, for every cell in your body is intelligent and responds to your divine directive. You have this ability as a Child of God. Step outside in the beauty of nature and look up to the sky, focus on the rays of light as they enter into your third eye, crown chakra, and every pore of your being. Invite the rays of light to heal, transform and awaken you to the multidimensional being you were meant to be. As you do so, you activate latent ancient codings and memories deep within your consciousness, assisting you with your realignment and healing process.

Pure LIGHT is your natural state of being... As you allow yourself to bask in the luminous reflection of who you are, you shine bright on humanity and light up the world, co-creating a new sense of peace, unity, and community of Spirit. Open the doorway of your soul and remember the Majestic Being that you are. As you answer the call of your internal song and honor the truth and light within your heart, you ILLUMINATE those souls awaiting to awaken... And so it is. I AM Aurora.

Affirmation: I AM the governing presence of Light.

> I AM in supreme and stellar health. Every single cell of my body is radiating in divine perfection now.

FREE WILL
THE
GIFT OF CHOICE

Every soul, upon divine timing, ignites the memories and keys within, activating the teachings they need to encourage expansion, and propel them forward on their journey into the light.

As you allow yourself to have a deeper understanding for others, you open the portal for Mass Consciousness to manifest more quickly on the planet.

The receptive nature of the human spirit allows one to open up to the Divinity of ALL Beings, thereby welcoming the uniqueness of every soul and their level of maturation on the spiritual plane.

As we have previously stated through our channel, subatomic molecular structure is based on particles or atoms combined with love and compassion of the human energy field. This unique combination is necessary to create the perfected light body, the ultimate spiritual vessel in this new dimensional reality. For those individuals who wish not to make the preparations and ascend in the Age of Light, all is not lost, for they too, have free will to choose what is best for their soul at this given time on the planet. These souls will simply be operating at a lesser frequency ~ only one outside of our dimensional range of motion, so to speak. We ask that you hold these beloveds in your hearts, send them light and divine love, and allow them to be where they are at this time. To many of you, this can be of alarming concern, as you are distraught over particular family members or loved ones not making this beautiful shift of alignment, but fear not Beloveds, for as your great Teacher Sananda has said, their Ascension will be just as their soul has planned and in accordance with their blueprint and divine purpose, growth, and maturation on the spiritual plane. Every soul here has been prompted to awaken, to ignite the memories and keys within, activating the resources they need to accelerate growth and evolution on the spiritual plane. So trust... and hold these souls close to your heart, for when you radiate the essence of love, joy and compassion to those around you, you strengthen the planet's energetic matrix and Bridge of Light.

We would like to add here that many of you Light Bearers have made the necessary spiritual contracts to awaken heartfelt souls and family members closer to the Eve of the grand Ascension, so these souls will be directly aligned with your energetic matrixes to make the great shift into the much awaited Heaven on Earth. I AM Aurora, beside the Beings of Light, guiding and assisting you always.

Affirmation: I AM sending light to my loved ones, and to all Beings everywhere.

I AM holding the energetic field of light for all Beings to awaken.

BE STILL
AND KNOW THAT
I AM GOD

It is the Higher Self, the still voice within, the Bright Inner Light, that is waiting to be discovered by EVERY soul in embodiment.

Be still and know that I AM GOD. Through stillness your questions shall be answered, for within the quiet space of your heart, I reside.

Beloveds, I ask that you take a deep breath and feel my presence in your heart. As you breath in and fill your heart with light, know that I AM there. Feel my love fill you up and encircle your entire Being through every cell of your body. I speak to you in the still moments of your day, in meditation and prayer, in joyful moments, and when you are drifting in and out of 'tween times just before awakening and sleeping. I bring you messages of hope and peace, for I AM with you. I live in the three-fold flame within your heart that is brightly lit, which nothing can extinguish...calm, patiently waiting for you to awaken to the light of KNOWINGNESS, for knowingness is the key to the ascended heart. As you merge with the coming waves of light and your beautiful planet integrates the energies of this New Age, I will remain by your side, for I dwell within you, in the Secret Chamber of your Heart, burning bright. Be not afraid My Children, as you are here to awaken to the light of knowingness that we are ONE. This is the promise that I have made unto you, and so it shall be. I shower you with blessings and love and await you at the Table of Plenty. I AM Sananda.

Affirmation: I AM one with God.

> I AM fully aligned and beautifully merged
> with the three-fold flame within my heart.

GUARDIANS
OF
LIGHT

You chose to be here at this exact time to hold the frequency
of LIGHT, to expand your vision of LOVE, and to assist as
Guardians of the planet. As you hold true to your ultimate
global vision for humanity, you broadcast a high vibrational
electromagnetic field that supports, transforms, and
nourishes ALL.

You have been the Way Showers, the Gatekeepers, the Guardians
of Light of this new dimensional frequency, and for that you
are honored immensely, for you have persevered through
treacherous storms, you have stayed the course through the
dark night of the soul, you have sustained ridicule and judgment
for your pioneering vision and inexhaustible efforts. At last your
reward is here. As Guardians of Light, you usher many souls
through these changing times, going back and forth through
the dimensional veil, for all souls are not ready to ignite their
flame of consciousness at the same time. You are the brave
warriors that proceed to the front line to make certain all is
ready. What joy we hold in our hearts as we have witnessed the
materialization of long last, the much foretold story of Mother
Earth's Ascension, and your role of assisting her from here
on out. We stand steady by your side and carry the Torch of

Light as we walk hand-in-hand into the new Era of Terra. I AM Aurora.

Affirmation: I AM a faithful Guardian of Light.

I AM filled with gratitude and joy, graciously receiving good in all areas of my life now.

COSMIC
AIRBORNE DIVISION

Cosmic Angels of Light and Silver Chariots in the sky.

From the Cosmic Airborne Division from which we operate, we sit at the right hand of The Most Radiant one, Sananda, most familiarly known to you as Master Jesus. He is the Exalted One and we honor and follow his command aboard his many star fleet ships, including our own. We are his Sky Ambassadors, if you will. He encourages us to spread the message of Love, for this is the energy that can save your precious planet which has come close to being dismantled many times at the reckless hands of man, missiles, and bombs. We are here to assist and guide you into the new millennium, and ask that you keep an open mind in the days to come, for we are kindred spirits of the earthlings, your Brothers and Sisters of Light, the Airborne version of the Great White Brotherhood. We are Cosmic Angels, Star People, but in a much more etheric form. Our energetic matrixes spin at an extreme rate making us invisible to your physical eye. There are certain clairvoyant beings that can detect us with precision of their third eye, or psychic eye, but in order for us to be seen by humanity, we must shift our frequency to a different caliber. This is when you see our silver chariots in the sky. We have now chosen to be detected, for we are here to be of great service in the coming days. We will be appearing more and more in the sky to your earthling race and look forward to the day when we stand side by side and communicate in the Light of Spirit for the good of humanity, and life on all planets throughout the Galaxies, for this is what The Golden Age has in store. Be not afraid, for we appear much as you do, quite humanesc, but shimmery, tall, thin, with light skin and hair. We teleport and travel in our starships or crafts. We communicate from our heart centers, telepathically, and through our eyes. When you see us, you will feel a calming sense of peace and love, for we are Beings of Light and Love, we are ONE with you. I AM Aurora and I bring you these messages of peace today.

Affirmation: I AM a clear channel of light and knowledge.

I AM seeing and communicating clearly with the Cosmic Beings of Light that guide me.

BE NOT AFRAID

Be not afraid. Embrace the Truth.

What we would like to share with you, Dear Ones, is that there have been forces of dark that have attempted to scare humanity through negative films and media, creating horrific aliens and reptiles coming from the sky through crafts and UFO's on the big screen, so to speak. The dark forces have attempted to paralyze the masses through fear to prevent a warm reception from us - the Sky Borne Command, Beings of Light, for we are not of those races. We have protected your planet for many many centuries from undue harm by many negative races and authority figures. We have detonated nuclear missiles, atoms and bombs to protect your planet's existence. We feel a deep connection to the human race and it is our urgent mission to assist in the long awaited Ascension of the planet. The Light has already won. We look forward to our most blessed reunion with our earth families. KNOW that your Star Families are near you always, protecting you, as they patiently await the joyful reunion. I AM Aurora of Light.

Affirmation: I AM releasing and clearing any fear and negativity from all levels of my beingness and my cellular memory now and forevermore.

I AM living the truth within my heart now.

EARTHLY
ANGELS

You are an INTERSTELLAR Traveler, here on Assignment to assist humanity's awakening and transition into The Golden Age of Light.

There are many members of our Sky Borne Division that are walking the earth, that look much like you, for they are specialists in assisting planets ascend. These earthly angels, some of whom are reading these pages, are helping mankind and the planet raise its consciousness and prepare for Ascension. These are the calm, patient, compassionate beings that commonly work in the healing, writing, music, and creative fields, though they are from all walks of life. Some are not fully awakened to the realization that they are from a higher dimensional plane, but will be attuned to this knowledge soon. For those that are aware, you can recognize them by a glow in their eyes, a peace in their hearts, a presence in their countenance. They love nature and animals; "Compassion" is their battle cry. These are souls that have graced the earth and planetary systems before, diligent members of the Allegiance of Light. They have taught, guided, and led the masses to bask in the frequency of Light and Self Realization, some for centuries. They have brought forth the principles of the I AM Presence and Higher Self, for when one REMEMBERS they are One with God, they bathe in the knowingness that all is possible, and they merge with the multifaceted jewel of the heart. I AM Aurora, I honor you deeply, and support you in your deep remembrance of Self.

Affirmation: I AM Remembering the ancientness of Who I AM and I AM creating my life anew.

I AM a receptacle of higher light knowledge.

DIVINE CONTRACTS
SACRED UNION

Your soul draws to you opportunities and circumstances that allow you to reach deeper levels of your Beingness for movement forward on your path.

Lets talk about Divine Contracts, Sacred Union: As earth inhabitants you desire to love and be loved. But, it is not so simple is it, Dear Ones? Each particular soul carries a unique frequency that broadcasts energy…you attract those souls that can learn and benefit from you, and that you have agreed to experience "soul contracts" with, long before you reincarnated into this lifetime. Visualize a big amphitheatre with a stage. At that pivotal moment before you choose what body you will incarnate and what lessons you will encounter to spiritually evolve into the super-conscious being that you are, a collection of souls appear in the audience, each eagerly waving their arms, volunteering to play certain parts in your life on this plane. They beg to be chosen… Some of the roles may be light, airy, and beautiful, and some may be dark and traumatic. But what is important to remember is that whomever the soul and whatever the circumstance, that soul chose the part at that precise moment, out of their love for you. It was their desire to assist you in embracing the light and to Remember Who You Are. The person who may have played the darkest, most challenging role, was actually a soul that loved you very much on a different plane, but understood the valued depth and severity of the turbulent role they would play in your life. We realize this is a lot to digest, especially for those who have experienced times of despair and trauma, but we promise you that one day, you will understand the great story and the meaning of this message. You will understand the Gift in the betrayal, loss, misinterpretation, or abuse that you sustained. I might also add here that the individuals playing these parts forget instantaneously upon their conception that they are here to play such a role. It's as if a delete button is pushed before exiting the birth canal. Just as each soul's memory bank is erased and cleared upon conception so they can begin anew to awaken and evolve, so is the recollection of your soul mates, sacred souls, and darkest challengers... Thus, it is the true journey of spirit to AWAKEN to the Light. To carry this Light like a radiant shield, illuminating all you meet. To REMEMBER that you are an Extraordinary Being, here to manifest the Glory of God within you, to LOVE one another, and assist Planet Earth in its most vital and long-anticipated Ascension process. Do not be weary, do not fret, as we are here to guide you every step of the way. I AM AURORA.

Affirmation: I AM a Radiant Being of Light here to manifest the Glory of God within.

I AM grateful for the experience of life lived fully and embrace the mission I AM here to fulfill.

BROADCASTERS
OF LIGHT

You are a powerful energy emitter in every waking and sleeping moment. Set your gauge to your highest light frequency.

When you begin to hold, keep and maintain higher dimensional frequency, you become a Broadcaster of Light. LIGHT, which is the energy of GOD, is the supreme intelligence of the Universe. As you maintain your Body of Light, you become a Conduit of Spirit, transmitting energy to all you meet and strengthening the Planetary Grid. When you act in the capacity of love and compassion and send light to others, you broadcast high frequency electromagnetic rays, healing hearts, and changing the vibration of the planet.

Beloveds, you are loved and illuminated by the light, for you are the Carriers of Light. You have agreed to be here at this particular time with your embers burning bright, to hold the frequency for humanity at this pivotal point of challenge and leap of consciousness on the planet. As you hold true to your mission of service, as you shine your light, pray, meditate, bless, you activate the true divine essence that is stored deep within the Secret Chamber of your heart, radiating your energy to all you meet, assisting mankind in awakening. As you transmit this bright light, you ignite dormant memories in those you meet, activating their deep recollection of Self, giving them permission to awaken to the Light of Spirit within the three-fold flame of their hearts, so that they too may carry this torch and assist others in their activation process. In eternal peace and love, I AM Aurora.

Affirmation: I AM a Broadcaster of higher dimensional Light.

I AM fully aligned with the Secret Chamber of my heart.

TEMPLE
OF TRANSPORT

Honor and respect your physical body, for it has a consciousness of its own and has served as your faithful port of call in this incarnation.

Your physical body is a gift from Creator and you have chosen this particular, unique embodiment to assist you through your journey on this plane. However, some have mistreated their bodies of flesh because they believe they are separate from the Source, and that they are not connected. Your body is your Temple of Transport and you must treat it with the utmost respect and honor. You are housing the multidimensional matrix that is you, your soul's blueprint, and your physical vessel has been through much as you have been educated in the Laws of Spirit. Honor, nourish, and respect this spiritual vessel and it will bring you great results in return. Fill your body with light and love. Spend time in nature, bask in the glory of things that make your heart sing. Commune with your physical vessel as if you were talking to a faithful friend. Look at your reflection in the mirror and tell yourself you are very loved. Thank your body for housing and carrying you through your most sacred journey on this plane. As you do so, you immerse yourself in light; you become a luminous being. I AM Aurora.

Affirmation: I AM honoring & nourishing my physical body now.

I AM grateful to my faithful port of call.

DO WHAT YOU
LOVE
LOVE WHAT YOU DO

Your innermost visions and dreams are downloads from your Higher Self, guiding you toward your soul's purpose. As you allow these Spirit-sanctioned energies to permeate the deepest corridors of your Beingness, you channel higher light frequency. Allow your Spirit to GLOW...

Your soul craves creative outlet. As you nurture that aspect of self, you become more fully aligned with your Higher Self, the Spark of God within.

Dear Beloveds, do you not feel yourselves GLOW when you bask in a creative endeavor or joyful activity that makes your heart sing? When you spend time doing what you *Love* to do, you fill your body with *Light*, and automatically become a Conductor of higher light energy. When you shine your spiritual light on everything you do, you nourish your soul and create infinite opportunities for immense growth and evolution into higher consciousness, activating your I AM Presence and awakening to your true potential. As you express your highest nature through those Spirit-guided activities you enjoy, you raise your vibration, and the frequency of the planet, strengthening the Crystalline Planetary Grid. This is why we encourage you to creatively self-express through your heart centers, and take time engaging in endeavors that bring you joy, peace, laughter, and contentment, for the universe constantly seeks a channel through which it can express itself. Allow your intention to encompass a greater understanding of your multidimensional self and the role you came here to fulfill on this planet, for you are a Divine Alchemist. You are a Living Master walking the Earth, and as you awaken to the Remembrance of Self and the immense gifts you are here to share with the world, you nourish your soul, becoming a Co-Creator of the world you wish to live in. In doing so, you light up the Earth, for the greatest gift you can give humanity, is to LIVE your LIGHT. The world is filled with wide open spaces…what Masterpiece will you create in yours? Through service and infinite love, I AM AURORA.

Affirmation: I AM blessed with infinite possibilities now.

I AM living my light & expressing my highest nature in all that I do.

MUTATIONAL
SYMPTOMS
IN
THE GOLDEN AGE

When you drop density and begin building your light body, you may experience interesting physical symptoms.

As your physical body begins to drop density, there are many changes that occur within your framework. One of the most common complaints as you begin to build your light body is flushing, or diarrhetic symptoms. You may suddenly have a four day period of cleansing the intestines at different intervals during this process, for as you raise your frequency, your vessel must interiorly realign. It is as if you are going through an internal "house cleaning", so to speak. Everything within your physical vessel is being recalibrated and realigned, similar to the tune-up or overhaul of an automobile. Other symptoms some may experience are dizziness, spinning, blurred vision, extreme fatigue, and headaches, to name a few. Your physical form needs time to integrate and assimilate these powerfully high vibrational energies that are streaming through your Beingness at an immense speed. You may feel dizzy or like the room is spinning when you stand up, lie down, or close your eyes. Fear not, for this is actually a very good sign that you are transmuting and transforming your vehicle into its higher dimensional state. There may be days when you feel as if you can't read or clear your vision, for the molecules, subparticles, and atoms that are rebuilding your inner matrix affect your vision markedly, due to the fact that the eyes have a very complex and pinpointed molecular makeup within the corneal vortex. You may feel like you suddenly have short term memory loss, to the point of walking across the room and not remembering where you were going or what you were doing. You may stop mid sentence, not able to form words... Remember, you are in a mutational process, you are restructuring. It's like an old house that has been stripped clean and is being remodeled. You may be feeling extremely exhausted no matter how much sleep you're getting. Again, all part of the divine upgrade. Not only are you channeling and anchoring the new energies onto the earth plane, but your energy system is also being readjusted and realigned while you sleep, for this is the time that you are bathed in stillness... It also allows the rebuild to "settle in" and merge with the interior makeup of your earthly vessel.

The electronics in your home or surrounding area may suddenly go haywire, or malfunction for no apparent reason. You may blow light bulbs and fuses. You may be driving under a street lamp and notice is goes out, only to look in your review mirror and see it flash back on. This is because as your frequency rises, you emit high velocity electromagnetic pulses that affect electronic gadgets in your energetic vicinity. As frustrating as this may seem, it is actually a fabulous sign that your vibration is very high. Try to see the humor and gift in it.

Additional symptoms we would like to include are severe occipital headaches at the base of your skull near the "Mouth of God". This is an extremely sensitive area on your vessel, located where your head sits on your spinal column, that channels higher light frequency, so if the pressure becomes too great, simply state, "Please deliver endorphins", and have your Etheric Healing Squad work on you in sleep time. Small episodes of racing heart, like butterfly wings, is also a common complaint during this transformational process. This is very brief, but can pull at your attention. The heart chakra is opening and expanding more fully in preparation for deeper communication through the heart center as multidimensional beings. A vacillation in blood cell counts may also occur during mutation. Your systems are changing constantly, and many of you have been recoding, reconnecting and reactivating your DNA back to its original structure for a long time now. So please, Dear Ones, have faith, and try not be alarmed by these temporary and interesting feelings, sensations and changes taking place in your physical vessels, for they too are in accordance with your cosmic upgrade and movement forward into your perfected light bodies. Added benefits of shifting into the light body are age reversal and disappearance of pain in the physical vessel.

(Please understand, Beloveds, it is not our intention to diagnose or give medical advice. We are simply explaining various physical sensations that may arise as you raise your vibration through your recalibration and realignment process, in preparation of merging more fully with your light bodies. We are not asking you to blatantly ignore extreme physical pain, for what we are speaking of is very short term and fleeting. If you are experiencing substantial, intense physical discomfort for *any* reason, we would encourage you to seek out assistance for appropriate health care monitoring.)

Affirmation: I AM recalibrating and realigning my energy system into my highest spiritual essence and divine blueprint now.

I AM upgrading my energy matrixes now.

INTEGRATING
COSMIC FREQUENCIES
SHOWERING THE PLANET

As you embrace the new waves of Cosmic Light Energy, you strengthen your nervous system and vibrational velocity, enabling you to download and assimilate a deeper clarity of purpose.

The cosmic stream of consciousness is unending and invites you to dive in and explore the limitless potential of Self...and therefore, Mankind.

As solar flares and eclipses continue to increase and bombard your planet with stepped up energy, your human vessels may experience an increased sensation of spinning or vertigo. This is because the solar flares and increased infusions of energy showering the earth plane cause your merkaba, the exterior energetic matrix that surrounds your physical vessel, to spin at an increased rate. An affirmation that is helpful at this time is, "I AM integrating and assimilating these high vibrational frequencies now!" We would also ask that you spend additional time in NATURE during the increased solar activity and walk the earth, preferably with the bare soles of your feet, for this will assist you in grounding in these powerful waves of light. You may also find it beneficial to meditate against a tree or spend extra time in your flower or vegetable gardens. Many highly sensitive Starseeds and Light Servers walk a labyrinth as an amazing intention for anchoring in these sometimes challenging streams of energy. For some of you, you may need to fully merge with these energies before going into a horizontal position at times of rest. Simply stating, "I AM beautifully merged with these high vibrational energies now", will assist you and lessen the spinning affect. Frankincense oil is also very beneficial with grounding in these new vibrational energies. We honor you for your diligent effort in anchoring in these sensational frequencies, for when you EMBODY the waves of light showering the earth, you become a precious link in the transformation of the planet. I AM Aurora and I serve you from my heart center, blessing each and every one of you today.

Affirmation: I AM integrating and assimilating these high vibrational frequencies now.

I AM fully aligned and beautifully merged with my merkabic field now.

ETHERIC
HEALING SQUAD

You each have an Angelic Healing Squad that assists you in your physical, emotional, and spiritual recalibration and healing, during your Ascension process.

Each of you reading these pages has come here to assist the planet in its transition, whether you consciously realize it or not. As such a member of the Earth Allegiance of Light, you are assigned an etheric healing team, or angelic healing squad, that works with you upon request. These are very loving Beings, a conglomeration of Angels, Star People, Ascended Masters, Elementals & other Cosmic Guides. We ask that when you are ready to go to sleep at night, you lay comfortably on your back with your arms at your side, and call in your etheric healing team. You will be presented with a name for this special group; do not judge it when it comes to you, it may be playful or serious; nevertheless, it will appear. Tell these Beings what is going on in your physical body, what hurts or aches, and what you would like them to heal. They do not need to hear specific diagnostic terms, as medical diagnosis imprints negative energy into your blueprint. Then THANK them! As you drift off to sleep, you will feel tingles and other airy sensations going on throughout your vessel. You may also feel your body begin to vibrate as if there's a fiber optic highway coursing through you. As Light Servers your systems need extra energy and attention due to all the grid work, anchoring in of energies and coding you provide to the planet and others each day. Some nights, you may want to ask for a good night's sleep and to feel rejuvenated and energized when you awaken. No request is too small or large, for these Beings have vowed to be at your service, in divine love and light, just as you have vowed to assist the planet. In adoration and service, I AM Aurora.

Affirmation: I AM grateful for my Angelic Healing Squad and thank them for returning me to my stellar health now.

I AM relaxed, rejuvenated and refreshed.
Every single cell in my body is vibrating in pristine perfection.

YOUR HEART
IS THE PORTAL OF
HIGHER DIMENSIONAL FREQUENCY

The light of your heart is the GATEWAY through which your Higher Self communicates.

Any time you think of someone with LOVE, you raise their level of light and you become an active link in strengthening the Planetary Grid. Your heart is the portal of higher dimensional knowledge and frequency. Each moment you think a loving, kind thought of someone, your heart center delivers a multifaceted matrix of light that acts as a messenger, streaming and expanding out to that individual, place or thing, creating a Bridge of Light, if you will. This frequency showers the recipient with unconditional love, upgrading their energetic field and matrix, raising their vibration. As they receive the rays of light and love, they feel drawn to send love to others, creating a larger matrix of light, bridging people, places, communities, cities, transforming the planet. So we would ask you to send love from your heart centers, whenever the thought arises, for this seemingly simple act will assist greatly in the transformation and Ascension of your Mother Earth. Send love to strangers you see walking the street; send love to the animals, domestic or wild; send love to your neighbors; send love to the cities you live in; to the world, for through the crystalline matrix of the bejeweled heart, the evolution of the planet begins to unfold.

So we ask you, our Beloved Ones, to fan the embers of love burning deep within your hearts... As you radiate this divine energy to the world, you redefine the Global Community of higher light frequency, and lovingly hold the field for mankind to REAWAKEN in The Golden Age. From the Solar Heart of Humanity, I bring you these messages today. I AM Aurora.

Affirmation: I AM beautifully aligned with the multifaceted jewel of the heart.

I AM expanding my heart center and sharing my LIGHT with all Beings everywhere!

YOU ARE A MULTIDIMENSIONAL BEING OF LIGHT

You are a Multidimensional Being here to evolve into your highest potential and contribute to the betterment of humanity through service and love. Many of you are specialists in assisting planets Ascend... Some of you have done it many times.

You are not forgotten, Beloved Ones. We salute you for remembering the journey, the path, for evolving into the Magnificent Spiritual Beings that you are through these tumultuous times on the planet, to get to this exact point, at this precise time, to remember the next step... Through service and love, you raise the frequency of humanity, it is as simple as that. There are many of you working in private, behind the scenes, assisting with the consciousness movement on the planet. We honor you for your unending dedication and service in this most diverse time and look forward to the days ahead when we will stand beside you as a Unified Nation of Brothers and Sisters of the Stars.

You are Multidimensional Beings here to emanate light and REMEMBER your assignment of duty on this plane as it emerges into the new Age of Aquarius, and to help carry those who have lost their way. There are many Warriors of Light who have yet to activate their inner memory, but in the interim, as you wear your badges of honor and go in behind the scenes to retrieve and awaken those that seem to have fallen through the cracks of the grid, your act of love and service is your valuable weapon, for it opens and ignites the ancient memory and matrix within their hearts, revealing to them *their* inner, magical, POWERFUL Being. I AM Aurora and I stand beside you in service and dedication on this day and always.

Affirmation: I AM a fully awakened, Multidimensional, Conscious Spiritual Being.

I AM a vessel of light, love, and divine service.

GALACTIC STAR
FAMILY

*Your Star Family of Light is around you and assists with the
planetary shift, anxiously awaiting your joyful reunion.*

Your Galactic Family of Light has not forgotten you, in fact,
we are in your very presence. We radiate with pride at all the
work you have done to REMEMBER who you are and step into
your soul mission on this plane, in preparation for the coming
Age of Light. We communicate with you through feelings of
loving energy, thoughts, creative insights, downloads, and
inspired moments, but most of all in your times of stillness.
We hear your cries of concern and despair; we feel your joy and
laughter. KNOW that we surround you in love, holding you in
the highest esteem, for you have chosen to be an active member
of the Unified Division of Light, holding the frequency for the
much anticipated Heaven on Earth.

We come to you as Star Fleets of Light, ever vigilant in our
crusade to save your most precious Planet Earth. We have been
by your side through the ages, but you have not seen us. We
walk beside you and fill your atmosphere with our sacred crafts
to patrol and protect you, for we are your Star Families of Light.
We serve beside Sananda, The Most Radiant One, in our mission
of peace on earth. In days to come, you will see us and what a
joyful occasion it will be, for we have long awaited our connection
in Spirit, to walk hand in hand with you, our beloved Brothers

and Sisters of Light, to live in peace and harmony in a world filled with love and in the divine glory of His name. The Heaven on Earth you have anticipated will make manifest, and you will be astounded by the beauty of Nature and the camaraderie of ALL life on the planet, for you will be ONE with All That Is. You have chosen the side of LIGHT and for that we applaud you greatly. The dark forces will soon be completely diminished from your planet and your DNA will be restored to its rightful, once pristine 12-strand, as you navigate in your perfected light bodies, your multidimensional selves, for you have chosen to be a time traveler in His name, and in His name you shall dwell.

Some of you have asked how you will know your Star Families when they arrive. We would like to tell you that we are already with you. We are of a high vibrational energy that emanates love, compassion and light. You will feel our love in your heart centers. You will have the sense that you are ONE with us and you may feel overwhelmed with emotion and weep, for your soul has long awaited our arrival. As previously stated through our channel, we appear very humanesc, but more ethereal, shimmery, we glow. We may also appear as "ORBS", which are floating, translucent spheres of light in different shapes and forms. We are fair skinned with fair hair and normally wear long white robes, but are sometimes in our galactic aviator apparel which appears as a uniform, with glowing emblems. Our palms radiate a violet light, which is the violet flame of Spirit. We will communicate to you through our heart centers which will emanate a bright light. You will also notice a bright light that radiates from our pineal gland, or third eye center of telepathic communication. We will speak to you as well through telepathy and our eyes. It will be a reunion of utmost joy and supreme remembrance. We hold the field for the comings days as you prepare for this disclosure, when your government officials take their needed steps so that we may decloak our starships and you may acknowledge us living and walking beside you. Until then, know that we surround you and embrace you always. In joyful anticipation and devotion, I AM Aurora.

Affirmation: I AM seeing and communicating clearly with my Star Family of Light now.

I AM a Majestic Being of Light.

BE AN
ANGEL AMONG US

Every time you Practice Kindness, Meditate, Pray, Bless, you RADIATE higher light frequency.

As you expand your thinking to SERVE humanity, you become highly attuned to God, your Buddha Nature, All That Is. As you practice kindness, you automatically become a vessel of divine service.

You are ALWAYS being taught in every moment, what you need for the next step on your journey. For the simplest act, performed in the totality of the moment, takes you exactly where you need to be. As you evolve spiritually and EMIT more Light, you strengthen the Cosmic Bridge, you BECOME your Higher Self...

Each time you perform an Act of Kindness, you strengthen the connective chain on the Planetary Grid and raise the frequency of humanity. We ask you, Children of Light, to reach out, be of service, extend a helping hand to those in need, for when you act with valor and compassion, you not only assist the soul in need, but you strengthen the Cosmic Grid and the vibration of humanity, all in accordance with the Ascension of your most precious Planet Earth. We ask you, "Do you not feel the joy it brings to assist another fellow Being or soul?" When you SERVE others, you emanate an immense light, creating an abundance of opportunities and good things, wherever you go. This in turn causes a ripple effect encouraging others to do the same, and the "kindness cycle" continues, healing self, humanity, the planet, the universe. I AM Aurora.

Affirmation: I AM a loving, compassionate humanitarian. My soul and my Higher Self are in perfect alignment in service to others.

I AM a precious link in strengthening the Bridge of Light.

GATEWAYS AND PORTALS
OF ENERGY

A part of you already exists in the higher dimensional plane you are preparing to ascend to, but you haven't fully realized it yet.

Some of you have asked about the new dimensional reality that Mother Earth will exist in... As we have shared with you in the past, there is no "light switch" moment, no particular date and time. What we would like to tell you is that you have already begun your emergence into The Golden Age. The frequency of your planet as it crosses the veil more fully into the Age of Light will be the 5th Dimension. Most of humanity is under the assumption that this is where the dimensions will stop for Mother Earth as she ascends into a star, however, this is not the case. The energies of high vibrational inhabitants and Earth will continue to build, layer upon layer, matrix upon matrix, and the planet will ultimately reside in the 7th Dimension of PURE love, Christ Consciousness and ONENESS. There are gateways and portals of supremely high velocity that will open up for inhabitants who choose to ascend on to this higher plane, but Planet Earth will never be a 3rd dimensional planet again. In service and love, I AM Aurora.

Affirmation: I AM easily and effortlessly navigating the portals of higher dimensional energy.

I AM a Conscious Spiritual Being living in my ascendency.

ANIMALS
AND LIGHT

Animals carry the frequency of LIGHT.

Your blessed animals encourage you to LOVE, for as you love, the frequency is raised in all humanity. We ask that you acknowledge the role the animals have come to fulfill on your planet. These precious 4-leggeds grace the plane to bring unconditional love to you, mankind, their families. They also serve as emotional buffers to those they adorn, so loyally absorbing and processing unbalanced emotional energies within the household. Some of these blessed beings go so far as to take on the illnesses of their earthly masters. Such a selfless act of love. When you acknowledge this unconditional gift of love, companionship, and commitment, you strengthen the Earth's grid. Much to the dismay of our Sky Borne Allegiance, animals are neglected and abused every day at the hands of man. This is not only devastatingly heartbreaking to the souls of these most precious pets that have chosen you as their earthen kin, but also to the planet, as this darkens the aura of man and lowers the vibration of Mother Earth. These animals also serve as Guardians of the earth plane, working steadfastly alongside Archangel Ariel, the Elementals, Dolphins and Whales. So embrace your beloved 4-leggeds, the precious ones that have chosen to journey with you on this plane of existence. Thank, honor, and LOVE them for the light, loyalty, and knowledge they so freely offer you through their loving, unconditional service and courage, for they have chosen YOU. Take the time to save or rescue a beloved animal in need. Acknowledge and validate these authentic souls for their planetary roles of Light Servers, for in doing so, you increase the frequency of humanity and brighten the aura of the planet. I AM Aurora of Light.

Affirmation: I AM in full gratitude to the beloved animals that have graced me with their presence.

I AM an advocate for the humane treatment of all creatures, great and small.

COSMIC
PRESENCE

Rejoice in the beauty of the beloved Celestial Beings that guide you.
If you only knew who walked beside you, you would never feel alone.

You are not alone... You are guided by countless souls in the higher dimensional atmosphere that have gone before you to lovingly light your path. The new Age of Ascension that your beloved planet is entering will be a place of PEACE, a place of Oneness, a place of Love and a place of Kindness. Feel the presence of your Brothers and Sisters of Light embrace you, feel our soft whisper of hope and encouragement in your hearts, feel us as we walk beside you in your day to day activities, for we are with you and we shower you with peace and guidance on this day and always. I AM Aurora.

Affirmation: I AM receiving Christed Cosmic Ascension
Blessings now.

I AM filled with peace, calmness, and serenity
of mind.

YOUR HEART CENTER
IS YOUR
VEHICLE OF TRANSPORT

Your HEART is your guiding light and navigator. Trust in your heart and your questions shall be answered.

It is there... The pure and peaceful state of Being, the ultimate TRUTH within your heart. Turn inward and bask in the effervescent Light of Spirit.

We speak of the multifaceted jewel of the heart, for through this heart center, you shall operate. It will be your vehicle of choice. This magnificent crystalline structure houses the codes and keys to your higher consciousness and multidimensional self. Once you have taken the vow to abide by Spirit and the Laws of the Universe in the coming Age of Light, the matrix within is activated, showering spheres of this Christed light energy across all space and time, and you become a sacred link in strengthening the Planetary Grid in preparation for the grand Ascension of your planet, which has already begun...

As you breathe in and feel the Golden Liquid Light within your heart GLOW, you raise your vibration, igniting this multifaceted matrix to expand through the Secret Chamber of your Heart, sending this unconditional love to all you meet. We ask that turn inward, into silence several times a day, for it awaits you, the sweet stillness within. As you turn the key and unlock your heart, you ignite the three-fold flame within. You BECOME your Higher Self, for it is in the quiet moments that you shall evolve and immerse yourself in the Presence of God. What an unparalleled act of love it is to sit within this stillness...to bear witness and listen to the sweet, subtle song of your inner voice. Through the doorway of silence, deep within you, is the spark of KNOWINGNESS that you are ONE. So we ask you to turn the key, unlock your heart, step inside, and roam the vast beautiful wilderness of your soul, where your field of joy awaits you. We Salute you on this day and always. I AM Aurora.

Affirmation: I AM communing with my wise inner being, my I AM Presence now.

I AM joyfully exploring the vast wilderness of my soul.

RELIGION,
POLITICS
AND MANIPULATION
OF THE SACRED BOOK

You are honored as Children of Light.

Beloveds, how dear you are, for you have steadfastly continued your journeys into the Light, through the mist of clouded and misperceived notions of the dark forces. You have stayed true to yourselves through the Light of Spirit, and your reward is coming as you merge with the Christed Cosmic Pillar of Divine Light and become one with your multifaceted, multidimensional true selves.

As we have brought through our channel before, when you choose love, peace, and equality, you are ONE with the Creator, Sananda, The Most Radiant One. Religion and politics have been misconstrued and misrepresented by the dark forces to invoke fear in the earthlings, in hopes that they could control the masses out of fear, shame and guilt. Spirit would never do such things to the Allegiance of Light, for Creator knows your roles on the planet and honors and cherishes every one of you reading these pages. The Illuminati and other dark forces have attempted to misinterpret your sacred teachings of long ago, and remold the sacred book into something it is not, through blatant revision and deletion of material in gigantic proportion, in order to impose fear and wreck havoc on the planet. We thank you for holding the field of light in your hearts. We know the journey has not been easy and we honor and pledge ourselves to your faithfulness in service, to walking the path, for we have reached a time when the final strand of the dark ones are leaving. The Light has prevailed and soon you will be free to stand hand-in-hand in the Light of Spirit with all living creatures in the frequency of harmony, love and equality for ALL, as the planet is cleansed forevermore of the dark forces. In faithful service, I AM Aurora.

Affirmation: I AM a faithful servant of the LIGHT.

I AM fully aligned with the Christed Cosmic Pillar of Divine Light now.

EMBRACE THE ROLE
YOU ARE HERE
TO FULFILL

You are a Magnificent Being of Light placed on the earth to make change and assist the planet's transition into The Golden Age.

You chose to be on the planet at this time as part of the Allegiance of Light, to assist humanity's healing and raise conscious awareness universally, in preparation for the Great Shift, The Golden Age of Light. Some of you may not be aware of your vow to fulfill such a contract, but it is promised in the days to come that you will REMEMBER your task, for you are Majestic Beings of Light, Living Masters walking the Earth. Some of you are Interstellar Travelers who have graced many planetary systems before, and you have volunteered to come here at this time to assist in this most crucial effort of Mother Earth as she makes her transition into a beautiful star. As Children of Light, you emanate light to all you meet, coding and activating filaments which have lain dormant deep within the beingness of every soul you encounter, preparing them to awaken and activate upon their divine timing in days to come. You are here to bridge the worlds for those ready to merge with ultimate knowingness. We honor your steadfastness, as the journey has not been easy for many who hold the Light of TRUTH within their hearts. You are revered, and the day is approaching when you will feel JOY in your hearts in *every* moment, like never before. It will be an unprecedented time on the planet, a new way of being for yourselves and Mother Earth, unequalled in the history of the Galaxies.

We so greatly honor you for your service and unwavering dedication in the role you came here to fulfill as you have so diligently assisted in the historical re-alignment of your beautiful planet. I AM Aurora.

Affirmation: I AM fulfilling my Divine Blueprint now.

I AM embracing my role as a Planetary Light Server now.

PERFECTED
LIGHT BODIES

As you anchor in higher light energies, you begin to build your Body of Light, activating dormant inner filaments which guide you to your soul's purpose and Remembrance of the Ancient Being that you are.

You are not simply your body or your brain, you are your SOUL...

As you evolve spiritually, your Body of Light GLOWS and vibrates at a higher velocity, radiating luminous light to those around you. This multi-crystalline structure of the human energy field contains millions of atoms and particles vibrating at the speed of light, inviting you to merge with your light body. Your perfected light body is immense, and as your begin to merge with the multidimensional sphere around you, the atoms, molecules, and subparticles begin to spin, activating your soul's merkaba to manufacture the speed you need to evolve into your highest dimensional state. This spinning vortex is capable of transporting you across time and space to anywhere you would like to go... it allows you to bi-locate to various places in time simultaneously. For now, you must work on building your Body of Light and holding this divine frequency so that you will be prepared when the time is near. Fill your body, mind, and spirit with loving thoughts and light, take care of your physical vessel, for soon you will be operating in your higher dimensional vehicle of choice. I AM Aurora and I bring you this message today.

Affirmation: I AM glowing in inner illumination.

I AM living in my perfected light body now.

AMBASSADORS
OF LIGHT

As you SHINE, Meditate, Pray, you become an Ambassador of Light in the evolutionary plan for humanity.

Each of you has come to this planet with a coded Blueprint to be a Bringer of Light and to assist in the transformation of Mother Earth as she makes her Ascension in the Great Shift...

Do not be pulled away and distracted by the chaotic energies of the world around you, Beloveds. We ask that you meditate, go into stillness and merge with the golden liquid light of consciousness, for here you will be bathed in the Light of Spirit.

There are many Light Bearers on your planet that have asked what they can do to assist in humanity's movement forward into The Golden Age. We ask that you go into stillness, meditate, pray, and fill your bodies with LIGHT. Send love and blessings to all people and beings everywhere, and to the planet. As you turn inward to the multifaceted jewel of the heart and listen to the murmur of your inner voice, you receive direction and guidance, for in that stillness is the whisper of God, ever present to guide you. Humanity has become distracted from Self through busyness and outside forces. It is time to turn inward to the quiet space within and bask in the glory of the Divine. As you operate from your heart center in all that you do, you raise your frequency, forming a matrix within that activates dormant filaments, emanating rays of light to all you meet. Take the time to be in silence, for through the chamber of your heart, progress will be made… Through the GATEWAY of your heart, you build your body of LIGHT.

We again remind you to spend time in NATURE, for nature holds the genetic ingredient to awakening through the rhythm of her loving heartbeat, grounding you into the infinite reality that we are ONE.

Wherever you go, whatever you do, send light from your heart to all you meet. It will raise the velocity of the recipient, you, and ultimately the planet. It is as simple as that, Dear Ones, for the Light of God transforms ALL. Those of you reading these words are already in the process of assisting in the transformation of the planet, for through these teachings you have been ignited and blessed as Creator's Eagles on Earth. I AM Aurora of Light, and I shower you with blessings today.

Affirmation: I AM speaking with the Voice of My Heart in each and every moment.

I AM radiating Light from my heart, wherever I go.

LIVE
YOUR LIGHT

Your Higher Self has a Master Plan for your life. Every experience you have ever had holds value and guides you to your Divine Blueprint. No experience is ever wasted.

All that you ENVISION already exists in the Spiritual Realm of the Universe... It holds the field, patiently waiting for you to remember the Tapestry you are here to weave...for that which you desire to be is already ALIVE within you. As you ignite your authentic vision, you become a co-creator of the New Earth.

You were born to Shimmer. Your soul is Infinite, and continually guides and nudges you in every moment to expand and glow in the immensity of the EXTRAORDINARY Being that you are, for the greatest gift you can give humanity is to Live your Light. As you ignite your ultimate vision of Self within, you shine your light bright on humanity and become a co-creator of the New Earth. When you begin to assimilate the realization that you came here for the education of Spirit and to master the evolutionary process of planet earth, you begin to receive Spirit-sanctioned downloads for your higher dimensional purpose on this plane. You manifest your infinite reality when you EMPOWER yourself to live your dreams. Every moment you are given on the earth plane is a GIFT. As you channel your highest expression of Self, you assist Mother Earth in her grand alignment and shift beyond the veil of The Golden Age.

All CREATION is manifested through thought form, light and sound. Our current macrocosmic reality requires you to explore the deeper understanding of Self, to identify your true nature and LIVE it in the world. As you live and share your immense talents with the universe, you transmute your energy to a higher vibrational state and automatically assist with the Ascension of the planet. And, as you shine your light to serve humanity, you become a precious link in strengthening the Planetary Grid. As you hear the call of your internal song and honor the truth within your heart, you LIVE your LIGHT and illuminate those souls awaiting to Awaken…you automatically serve others. And so it is, I AM Aurora.

Affirmation: I AM activating my ultimate vision now.

I AM living in my highest potential in each and every moment.

SEE
THE SPARK OF GOD
IN ALL LIVING THINGS

Every soul you encounter came here with the initial intent to AWAKEN and evolve into a Higher Dimensional Being.

As we traverse the Golden Age energies, humanity is required to embrace the uniqueness of ALL Beings, joining together in a unified Global cause. As you hold true to your highest vision for the planet, you broadcast an electromagnetic field that supports, transforms and nourishes ALL.

Dear Ones, we ask that you love all your Brothers and Sisters of Light, for they too have vowed to come to this plane and awaken to the Light of Spirit. As we cross the veil into Ascension, more and more souls will be igniting their divine memory of self, revealing to them what they came here to REMEMBER. As you see the Spark of God in all living things, you awaken to the higher dimensional frequency of who you are and your multifaceted soul emerges, casting light on all around you, allowing and giving others permission to embrace their memory of self and duty on this plane. We again ask you to live in harmony with all of God's creatures, for every species on earth serves a purpose for you and mirrors back what you need to SEE. Share your light and knowledge with those you encounter... Every soul you meet, no matter what the circumstance, is here to offer you a clue in your spiritual evolution. So judge not, Children of Light, instead lend a helping hand, shower light on all creatures great and small, and practice kindness always, for every soul here has come to find FREEDOM in the Light of Spirit. I AM Aurora.

Affirmation: I AM a Beacon of Light to all I meet.

I AM seeing the Spark of God in all living things.

YOUR WORDS
CREATE YOUR REALITY

Embrace the Power of the SPOKEN WORD. What you say creates a coded imprint and emblazes and overlays your energy field with a positive or negative result.

Beloveds, your words are the Trumpet of God, and continually create your present and future reality in this new vibrational frequency. The manifestational vortex of energy that is opening up on your planet is merged and aligned with the Christed Cosmic energy of light, so all that you think and say places your intention in the cyclic ordering from the Universal menu, so to speak. We would add here to be aware that every single thought affects every cell in your body, as it streams through your nervous system, creating either strength and vitality or weakness to your vessel. We ask you to remember...you place your order in every moment. Be aware of your power and ability to manifest all the desires of your heart. Use your metaphysical wands wisely, for in the coming years as The Golden Age progresses and continues to emerge in the higher dimensional atmosphere, your reality will be created instantaneously with mere thought. Your multidimensional vehicles will be in pristine mechanical order and you will have the ability to create into fruition all that is in accordance with the highest good of all. So in the coming days, we ask you to prepare. Center yourselves, speak, act, and operate from the highest place in your heart, for the way of the heart is the way of the future on Grand Terra, after your magnificent Mother Earth has made her shift. Your hearts will sing with the bright light and glowing embers of Spirit, and you will wear well-lit crowns of glory on your heads, for your spiritual centers associated with your psychic vision and wisdom will be activated and operating like a well-lit craft. The first step is to master the *Compass of the Heart*, for the heart is the guiding light and navigator. I AM Aurora.

Affirmation: I AM trusting the Compass of my Heart.

I AM allowing the Compass of my Heart to navigate me in each and every moment.

LINEAR TIME
A THING OF THE PAST

As you integrate the new spherical energies permeating the Earth, your multidimensional faculties expand. You become ONE with your Body of Light.

The essence of time is an interesting thing, is it not, for as you begin to shift into your perfected light bodies, you begin to lose track of linear reality as you know it. At this juncture on your planet, you are in an in-between state of being. One minute you may feel like things are progressing so rapidly that it's hard to keep up. Yet in the next moment, you may feel you have entered a time warp, or worm hole of space where everything slows down, as if you have pierced the dimensional bubble and are in an ethereal holding pattern of sorts... This is because at this point in time, you are straddling the energies of both realities, and all is suspended. It is in the spherical timeframe that the higher dimensional Beings reside, alongside The Most Radiant One as Celestial Angels and Cosmic Guides. On Earth, you are currently in between these energetic matrixes. But in the days ahead, it will become more clear that you have bridged the gap and your existence will begin to build and merge in the higher realms of the Galaxies. As you ride these elevated waves of light, you will experience more joy, peace, and love in your world, so we would ask that you embrace these waves of energy showering the earth, for as you do so, you become a magnet for higher consciousness.

As you integrate the new spherical energies saturating the earth, you expand your spiritual vessel preparing you for deeper emergence into The Golden Age of Light. Your multifaceted faculties will expand and you will be guided more fully into your planetary role. As you transcend linear time, you raise your vibrational stature and exist in a stepped up frequency, which allows you to more easily manifest your highest vision of self and ultimate vision for mankind. As you trust the insights you receive, you broaden the portal of cosmic knowledge and become a Conductor of this new spherical energy. The heartbeat of your multidimensional soul quickens and glows and you lovingly welcome your remembrance of self and your planetary role. For now, we ask you to keep building your Body of Light and know that we stand by your side, lifting you up in all that you do, for we are ONE and have vowed to lovingly assist you as your dedicated Team of Light in the coming age of the New Earth, where we shall reside together joyfully in the Kingdom of The Most Radiant One. I AM Aurora.

Affirmation: I AM living in spherical time now.

I AM in perfect balance physically, psychically and spiritually.

MESSAGES
OF HOPE

We reach you through song when you are unaware of it.

HARK THE HERALD ANGELS SING

Our messages come through many channels in a variety of ways, in our hopes to assist humanity. Where there is a pure heart and strong light, there is receptivity and openness to receive. For centuries we have been at your side... We ask that you listen to the lyrics of a popular Christmas classic, *"Hark the Harold Angels Sing"*, for through this song, we have also spoken to you through the ages. The "Herald Angels" are the Cosmic Angels, Sky Ambassadors, assisting in bringing you peace on earth... *Hark the Herald Angels sing, Glory to the newborn King, Peace on Earth and mercy mild...* We hope to reach mankind in preparation of the events which are soon to pass. The Most Radiant One is celebrated in the sky and we bring a new Peace upon Earth. *Joyful all ye nations rise; Join the triumph of the skies...* For it is through this song that we speak of the coming age, the rise of humanity, and the transition of Mother Earth in the Great Shift, The Golden Age of Light; the nations of people shall rise in peace and the Ascension is the triumph in the skies! Our messages are all around you. Listen and hear our guidance. Seek and you shall find, be still and know that you are guided always. I AM Aurora.

AGE OF AQUARIUS/LET THE SUNSHINE IN

While we seem to be in verse, we would also like to bring your attention to a most popular song written decades ago, that also presents beautiful information for the human race through lyric. As popular songs reach the masses and the words are sung, the throat chakra expands, amplifying the energy of intent, causing a ripple effect, and the transformation begins. The supremely majestic "Age of Aquarius/Let the Sunshine In" music medley does just that in its message and promise of peace to humanity. *When the moon is in the 7ᵗʰ house and Jupiter aligns with Mars, then peace will guide the planet and love will steer the stars...* This is very well put, as the planetary alignment supports the shift into The Golden Age and beyond. There will be harmony and peace on earth and LOVE will be the movement that transforms the earth, as you operate from your heart centers for the good of ALL. *This is the dawning of the Age of Aquarius, Age of Aquarius, Aquarius...* The dawning of the Age of Aquarius, the New Age of Light, The Golden Age which ushers in a new era of consciousness, brotherly love and humanitarianism. *Harmony and understanding, sympathy and trust abounding, no more falsehoods or derisions...* There is a new peace on earth, universal harmony through the Galaxies, and love for all living things, all Beings. There is no more hatred, fear, darkness, warfare, or manipulation by people of power. *Mystic, crystal revelation and the mind's true liberation...* The individual nations will fade and mankind will join together as ONE people. The inhabitants of earth shall awaken to their multidimensional selves and the power will be restored within their Beingness, healing the hearts and minds of all. *LET THE SUNSHINE IN... LET THE SUNSHINE IN... THE SUNSHINE IN... Open up your heart and let it shine on in...* This message could not make us happier as we are the Sky Borne Ambassadors that patrol and protect your planet steadfastly, near the Great Central Sun. We sit at the right hand of The Most Radiant One, and bring you these messages of love, peace, and hope, saluting you ALWAYS, I AM Aurora.

*"Hark the Harold Angels Sing" written by Charles Wesley in 1739.

*"The Age of Aquarius/Let the Sunshine In" medley written by James Rado, Gerome Ragni (lyrics) & Galt MacDermot (music) in 1967. Album released and performed by The 5th Dimension in 1969.

GALACTIC
INTERVENTION

LOVE is the Universal Password.

Open your hearts and give gratitude to the beautiful Beings who have assisted the earth in opening and reactivating the Cosmic Crystalline Grid of Light.

We bring you messages of PEACE and LOVE as the Airborne Division of the Great White Brotherhood, but it is also our responsibility to keep you advised and protected ALWAYS. Many have asked why the government officials that are in positions of authority to declare that our silver chariots are CHRISTED and in harmony and service to the planet, have not yet disclosed this truth. It is here. The time is now. Do not be in fear, Dear Ones, for everything is in divine accordance with the Laws of Spirit, the conditions of the earth cannot simply go on as they have for centuries without the horrific travesty that would have befell the planet had the Sky Borne Division and Christed ET's not intervened. We ask you to always embrace the light, do not be afraid, for fear will slow down the planetary process and prevent movement forward. We will always appear in the LIGHT and you will feel our love, compassion and serenity radiating from our energy fields. All that we ask of you is to stay calm, embrace the light, and guide others around you. There are those on your planet that are not ready to make this leap of trust and that is not to be judged, for they too, will have the opportunity to bask in the Light of Spirit at another time. For now, we ask that you fill your bodies with LIGHT, send LIGHT to all you know, including your blessed Mother Earth.

The new waves of energy that are showering your planet bring the ultimate level of peace and joy for Mankind. Love will be the universal password and the energy of Light will be experienced at a level never before achieved. It is through the Heart Center that you will communicate in Spirit, and the days of mental and emotional upheaval will be over. We are here in Love and Service, as your protective Cosmic Legions of Light through Aurora.

Affirmation: I AM embracing the Light and communicating with the Voice of my Heart now.

I AM in full gratitude to the Celestial Beings that guide and protect me always.

NOTHING LESS THAN
LOVE
WILL EXIST IN THE
NEW DIMENSIONAL ENERGY

LOVE is transformational and flows through the deepest canals of your Being...

We ask you to feel the love in your hearts, Beloveds, for it is through this portal that your illumination and ascension shall begin. This precious, multifaceted jewel within the Secret Chamber of your heart has waited many lifetimes to fully merge with the Light of Spirit, to commune with the I AM Presence, to at last become ONE with the Christ Conscious flame. Dear Ones, it is for you to LOVE one another, to show others the light you so gloriously carry within yourselves, for when you speak, they listen, and through your voice and words they find their way. As you evolve spiritually and allow your inner being to shine, you become a sacred element in raising the frequency of the planet.

LOVE is the most powerful force in the Universe and what we would like to tell you today is that through love, the earth will make its shift into its grand alignment in the stars. Through love, all things will be healed, and through love, you shall save your beloved planet, and the history of the Galaxies shall be rewritten forevermore. To watch the innocence and beauty of the children on your planet as they so effortlessly love and play, ever trusting and open, is to see the new horizon in The Golden Age of Heaven on Earth.

Love is transformational, it moves through the deepest corridors of your Being, saturating every cell of your body, then radiates outward. Nothing less than LOVE will exist in the new dimensional energies that will bathe your planet in its refurbished state of higher consciousness. Nature has attempted to share this sacred knowledge with mankind through the ages, but its attempt has fallen upon deaf ears. We ask that you open your hearts and minds and look at what nature has so graciously laid out before you, for through this incomparable vision, you will be transformed. Too numerous to mention, nature has demonstrated miracle upon miracle in the frequency of divine love. The penguin has brought us endless messages of patience, unwavering faith and love as it so carefully cradles its egg slowly and tenderly, inch by inch, across miles of arctic terrain to safe ground. The whales and dolphins have continually showered the planet with their unconditional frequency of love, as Record Keepers and Guardians of the planet, only to be hunted and slaughtered at the hands of man. These precious, blissful Beings of divine intelligence and love are the vibrational stewards of the Earth, embodying the stellar energetic frequencies that the planet will return to. They grace your plane from another star system to fulfill their duty in assisting humanity's emergence into the new Age of Light. They reside in the 11th dimension, and have sacrificed their existence to guide your planet, working diligently to repair and rebuild the electromagnetic grid. It is time for humanity to awaken to the cries of the innocent, to SEE the spark of God in all living things... When you open your heart to this realization, you begin living in the glorious new Era of Terra, the new Heaven on Earth, where there will be peace and harmony among all living things, wild and domestic.

The Elemental Kingdom and Nature Spirits also work hand in hand with our Sky Borne Division of the Great White Brotherhood, alongside Ariel and Uriel. They speak to you through the leaves and trees, and through the whispering winds of nature, always assisting and navigating. They also serve as Guardians and Protectors of the four-leggeds. So please, take the time to BE STILL in nature, to love all of God's creatures, and to embrace the feelings within your heart, for through the heart opening, awakening occurs.

For those of you who are leaders in the galactic field walking the earth, we ask that you hold in your hearts, those fellow brothers and sisters on the planet who have not yet mastered your level of knowledge. It may seem challenging at times to walk beside those earthlings that have not yet activated, but as you remember, you have vowed to come to the planet to assist in their ignition of Spirit. We understand your task has seemed insurmountable at times and that you have had to wade through spells of darkness, but alas, your reward is near in the days to follow for your diligence in duty. We love you and salute you, always. I AM Aurora.

Affirmation: I AM a faithful steward of the Planet.

I AM seeing the Spark of God in all living things.

YOU ARE
NOT FORGOTTEN

You are an Intergalactic Traveler here on Assignment to transform the frequency of Planet Earth...hold true to your vision of service.

Above all, you are LOVED... If you could only know how much love there is for you in the higher realms, you would never feel alone. As you take a deep breath and go into stillness, you feel our presence and the answer is clear. Your path is lit. We have felt your hope, we have felt your pain, we have felt your frustration of living in the physical plane, but not being OF it. There are many of you who have vowed to come here from other spaces in time, from other planets and Galaxies, to assist in fulfilling the destiny of Earth. There have been times when you have felt loneliness and despair to the depth and core of your Being. You have felt like an outsider, like no one else understood the complex origin of your weathered soul. You have yearned to return to your original place of origin, to your beloved planet, but you have prevailed, and your mission is in divine accordance with what your soul intended to do in this lifetime, for you are the Way Showers, the Light Servers, and the beautiful Starseeds from different Galactic Nations, who have so selflessly volunteered your incarnations to assist the Earth in its most memorable and urgent transition into the light. You are not forgotten and are never alone, Dear Ones... The Angelic Legions surround you, softly whispering in your ear and enfolding you in their blanket of loving care. We honor and celebrate you in the celestial realms, and hold the Torch of Light for you in our hearts, always guiding and loving you. I AM Aurora.

Affirmation: I AM a luminous Being of Light.

I AM an Interstellar Traveler fulfilling my purpose on this plane now.

THE
MAGIC
YOU SEEK
LIES WITHIN YOU

Nurture your INNER LIGHT... As you keep the embers burning in the deepest recesses of your Being, you Awaken to your soul's fullest potential. As you TRUST the insights you receive, you realize there is a divine purpose to everything around you, and that you are guided and directed ALWAYS.

You are here to Awaken to the Light of Spirit, to REMEMBER your grand and significant purpose on this plane, and to assist the Earth's evolutionary process. All that you need to know is deep within you... In this lifetime, it is for you to Remember Who You Are and ignite your unique planetary role.

Beloved Ones, all the knowledge and validation that you so readily seek lies within you. We ask that you sit in stillness, for meditation is the practice of accessing the LIGHT within, of allowing your inner being to bask in the infinite essence of Oneness, to evolve and grow... Even the briefest moment of silence connects you to the Totality of the Present, the sacred space within where you experience the Presence of God. As you meditate, you raise your vibrational frequency, strengthening your connection to your Higher Self and the

Celestial Beings that work with you. Take in a deep breath of pure crystalline white light and allow this powerful source to permeate your heart center and vessel. As you do so, every cell in your body is saturated and bathed in this divine liquid light. Visualize yourself filling every atom of your body with this beautiful light allowing the molecules, subparticles, and light filaments to merge, creating a divine KNOWINGNESS and wholeness within you. For all that you have sought, all that you desire, all that you aspire to be, has always been within your reach. Each of you has a divine soul purpose or spiritual mission, if you will. You each chose to be on beloved Mother Earth at this time to awaken to the ultimate realization that you are ONE with GOD. You have never been anything less. However, when you chose your incarnation into this lifetime, the tangible memory of your soul's blueprint was erased and you have spent this time as an Initiate wandering and weaving your unique tapestry into the ornate, intricate lifetime you have lived, ALL to get to this *exact point*... To ignite the memory within and to REMEMBER you are a powerful source of Light, here to make change and assist your precious planet in its crucial transformation. You embody the codes and keys of higher spiritual realization, so turn inward Dear Ones, practice stillness and listen to the sweet murmur within, for the Light of the Heart is the GATEWAY through which your Higher Self communicates. The path is lit and always has been. What you SEEK is inside of yourself. As you take time to commune with your I AM Presence, you discover a multitude of dimensional doorways, revealing infinite knowledge and love for you. Activate your divine blueprint and follow your inner gauge. Trust in your heart and your questions shall be answered. I sit beside Sananda, The Most Radiant One, and assist him in guiding the Solar Star Fleets surrounding you, holding the field for you to awaken. I am here of service and assist you always. I AM Aurora.

Affirmation: I AM fulfilling my spiritual mission now.

I AM one with my Higher Self and am remembering the role I AM here to fulfill.

ENERGY BLESSINGS
FROM
THE STARS

Lift up your hearts.

Beloveds, from the Sky Borne Division of the Great White Brotherhood, beside The Most Radiant One and Aurora of Light, we cradle you in our arms. We applaud you for your tenacious dedication on the path and salute you for taking your position in the front line as you have been activated and called to duty in this coming Age of Glory. The energies you will integrate as you cross the veil into The Golden Age and traverse through the multidimensional matrixes of light, recalibrate and realign your vessels through the multifaceted crystalline structures within the Secret Chamber of your Heart. We are here in service as your Brothers and Sisters of Light, available at any time to infuse your bodies with energy blessings from the stars. Ask and you shall receive, Dear Ones, open up to the pure infusion of White Light and your systems will be upgraded and purified. As you receive these Ascension Blessings, the multifaceted jewel of the heart activates at an ancient core level. Everywhere you go, everyone you meet, will feel the effervescent Light of Spirit around you, as you emanate your newfound frequency, expanding and awakening the hearts and minds of those you meet. Lift up your hearts for it is right to give thanks and praise... We are the Beings of Light and Aurora.

Affirmation: I AM receiving Energy Blessings from the
        Stars now.

        I AM receiving Ascension Blessings now.

AWAKEN
THE
VIOLET FLAME

The curriculum of Planet Earth is to learn, experience, and share the frequency of Love and Light.

The Light of your Heart is the PORTAL through which your Higher Self communicates. As you awaken to the light of consciousness, you begin to remember the Great Story and realize your life is for the education of Spirit, and that your evolution assists the planet greatly. As you step into this divine epiphany, you activate the violet flame within your heart, creating an elaborate energetic matrix that spirals and emanates outward, healing and transforming the energy of ALL living things. As you share this light with others, you ignite the memory of long ago within THEIR hearts, so that they too may awaken to the Light of Spirit and soar freely on their path of knowingness.

We would invite you to absorb yourselves in the I AM teachings of the Sky Borne Division and The Most Radiant One, for through these sacred decrees you shall transform your energy, and expand your Body of Light. Many of you reading these pages are already Keepers of the Flame, for you hold the violet flame of spiritual transmutation within your hearts. You serve as Beacons of Light to many, transforming the planet wherever you go. We assist all who wish to make this leap of consciousness through the Decrees of Light. As you chant the I AM affirmations, you touch the heart of Mother Earth and the Solar Heart of Humanity. You expand your Body of Light, thereby assisting the planet as she cleanses and merges into the energies of the new Era of Terra, creating Heaven on Earth for humanity, beyond the veil of The Golden Age. I AM Aurora.

Affirmation: I AM a Keeper of the Violet Flame.

I AM ONE with divine consciousness.

ALL
IS POSSIBLE

Invoke the Mighty I AM Presence...

Have faith, Dear Ones, for through His name, all is possible.

The I AM Presence knocks on the doorway of your heart, patiently awaiting an invitation to ignite the Spark of Divinity within. Every time you state I AM, you summon God into motion, for within each of you resides the I AM Presence, the Spark of Divinity, your Higher Self, which enables you to co-create with God, all that you desire. Do you feel the truth deep within your beingness as you read these words, for this has been the biggest spiritual secret, known by few mystics, prophets, and seers through the ages... God is not some distant figurehead as many organized religions would have the masses believe... The secret is, YOU ARE GOD. You are God... This Spark of God within you, your Higher Self, your I AM Presence is the commanding guiding navigator of everything in your life. And because you are One with God, you are the creator of your reality. The seeds of consciousness are activated when the awakening soul opens up to the understanding that they are ONE with God, not separate from the Source. You are at the helm, so to speak, of your greatest dreams and visions. We understand that when you initially hear this, the realization may seem somewhat self righteous and may even startle you, but as you affirm, "I

AM One with God", you will feel the envelopment of White Light and Truth deep within your heart. We would ask that you joyfully claim this newfound birthright, for in doing so, you will experience tremendous peace, joy, compassion, love, and illumination.

We would recommend that you work diligently on becoming a master of your thoughts and words as well, Beloveds, for the power of the spoken word is immense. Every time you utter or think a negative or damaging thought about yourself, you destruct and dismantle the I AM Presence within. Doubt erases your intuition and intention, and dampens the I AM Spirit, building a stone-clad fortress around your consciousness, limiting the conduit of light between you and Universal cosmic energy. We would further invite you to explore the possibility, that whatever appears to be a challenge in your life, may actually be the manifestation of your consciousness or thought forms, Dear Ones... for as you think, so shall you become. We would, therefore, encourage you to "rearrange" your thoughts to be flooded with images and impressions of the ideals that you wish to attain, experience, and achieve, for your mind is *Emblazed* with an imprint of all you believe to be true...

Fill your cup with the I AM Teachings, the "Elixers of Light" and you will not only transform yourselves, but everyone you encounter, for you will illuminate the world with the Violet Flame of Spiritual Transmutation that permeates every cell of your Beingness.

Emblaze these teachings into your consciousness, Beloveds, for they will unlock the Secret Chamber within your Heart and ignite your vessel for Ascension, as you soar into the energies of the New Earth. And so it is. I AM Aurora, beside the Beings of Light, and my beloved St. Germain, and we bring you these messages today.

Affirmation: I AM one with God.

I AM a Master of my thoughts in each and every moment.

I AM
DECREES

Beloveds, the following affirmations are a mere sampling that we offer you. We would ask that you repeat the affirmations that resonate with your heart and soul daily, for the decrees will shift your frequency instantaneously. We would also encourage you to create your own affirmations. State your intentions and *bathe* them in love... You may choose to chant or sing your affirmations, for the beauty of the emotional force assists with the deep intention of your decrees and is delightful to the Celestial Beings in the Spiritual and Angelic Kingdom. Through adoration and service, I AM Aurora.

I AM one with God.
I AM THAT I AM.

I AM one with my Higher Self.
I AM THAT I AM.

I AM fulfilling my spiritual mission now.
I AM THAT I AM.

I AM flooding my body with Christed Cosmic White Light now.
I AM THAT I AM.

I AM integrating and assimilating the cosmic waves of Light showering the planet now.
I AM THAT I AM.

I AM anchoring in higher light frequency now.
I AM THAT I AM.

I AM building my Body of Light now.
I AM THAT I AM.

I AM fully aligned and beautifully merged with the Christed Cosmic Pillar of Divine Light now.
I AM THAT I AM.

I AM recalibrating and realigning my energy system into my highest spiritual essence and Divine Blueprint now.
I AM THAT I AM.

I AM upgrading my energy matrixes now.
I AM THAT I AM.

I AM filling every single cell of my body with Christed Cosmic White Light and I AM surrounding myself with this White Light protection and the Golden Light of the Pyramid now.
I AM THAT I AM.

I AM activating and living my Divine Blueprint now.
I AM THAT I AM.

I AM a faithful Servant of Light.
I AM THAT I AM.

I AM beautifully aligned with the three-fold flame within my heart.
I AM THAT I AM.

I AM a magnet of higher consciousness.
I AM THAT I AM.

I AM activating my spiritual crystalline structures now.
I AM THAT I AM.

I AM releasing and clearing any & all fear and negativity from ALL levels of my beingness & my cellular memory now and forevermore.
I AM THAT I AM.

I AM a Temple of Living Light.
I AM THAT I AM.

I AM in supreme and stellar health now.
I AM THAT I AM.

I AM a Keeper of the Violet Flame.
I AM THAT I AM.

I AM living in my perfected Light Body now.
I AM THAT I AM.

I AM fully aligned with the Christ Consciousness Grid now.
I AM THAT I AM.

I AM one with God and ALL of Creation.
I AM THAT I AM.

I AM graciously receiving good in all areas of my life now.
I AM THAT I AM.

I AM vibrating in my highest frequency & truth in each and every moment.
I AM THAT I AM.

I AM a vessel of light, love and divine service.
I AM THAT I AM.

I AM a Beloved Child of God. I Love myself, I Know myself, I Trust myself, I BELIEVE in myself.
I AM THAT I AM.

I AM remembering the ancientness of Who I AM, and I AM creating my life anew.
I AM THAT I AM.

I AM living in my highest potential now.
I AM THAT I AM.

I AM receiving Energy Blessings from the stars now.
I AM THAT I AM.

I AM the perfect picture of health. I AM pristinely balanced physically, emotionally, mentally, spiritually, and cellularly.
I AM THAT I AM.

I AM recoding, reconnecting & reactivating my 12-strand DNA now.
I AM THAT I AM.

I AM a receptacle of higher light frequency.
I AM THAT I AM.

I AM communicating clearly with all of my enlightened Angels, Guides, Ascended Masters & Teachers, Divine Beings of Light, Nature Devas & Spirits, Christed ET's, and my Star Family of Light that guides me now.
I AM THAT I AM.

I AM a clear channel of Light.
I AM THAT I AM.

I AM speaking with the Voice of my Heart in each and every moment.
I AM THAT I AM.

I AM receiving Christed Cosmic Ascension Blessings now.
I AM THAT I AM.

I AM a joyful Steward of Mother Earth.
I AM THAT I AM.

I AM allowing the Compass of my Heart to guide me now.
I AM THAT I AM.

I AM a Magnificent Being of Light.
I AM THAT I AM.

I AM in perfect alignment with my Higher Self in service to others.
I AM THAT I AM.

I AM living in spherical time now.
I AM THAT I AM.

I AM infused with love and good nature and I AM sharing this energy with the world now.
I AM THAT I AM.

I AM Blessed with infinite possibilities now.
I AM THAT I AM.

I AM receiving Light Showers from the Ascended Masters and Beings of Light now.
I AM THAT I AM.

I AM a Divine Alchemist.
I AM THAT I AM.

I AM bathed in the Golden Liquid Light of healing now.
I AM THAT I AM.

I AM overflowing with Infinite Love, Grace & Kindness now.
I AM THAT I AM.

I AM living my Light in each and every moment.
I AM THAT I AM.

I AM fully aligned and beautifully merged with the Celestial Matrix of the Universe now.
I AM THAT I AM.

I AM co-creating with Spirit and manifesting miracles in my life now.
I AM THAT I AM.

I AM embracing & communicating with my Galactic Family of Light now.
I AM THAT I AM.

I AM glowing in inner ILLUMINATION now.
I AM THAT I AM.

I AM utilizing my spiritual gifts to assist humanity's healing and raise conscious awareness Universally.
I AM THAT I AM.

I AM embracing my role as a Planetary Light Server now.
I AM THAT I AM.

I AM love, I AM light, I AM wholeness, I AM clarity, I AM inner truth.
I AM THAT I AM.

I AM a Living Master walking the Earth.
I AM THAT I AM.

I AM Being, I AM Knowing, I AM Allowing, I AM Receiving.
I AM THAT I AM.

I AM living in my Highest Consciousness now.
I AM THAT I AM.

I AM filled with Gratitude and Joy, knowing good things come to me now.
I AM THAT I AM.

I AM a Beacon of Light and Love.
I AM THAT I AM.

I AM a Conscious Spiritual Being living in my Ascendency now.
I AM THAT I AM.

I AM radiating light and love to all Beings everywhere. The world is at PEACE and in perfect harmony now.
I AM THAT I AM.

I AM grateful for all that I AM.
I AM THAT I AM.

I AM THAT I AM.

YOUR WORD
IS YOUR WAND

Instantaneous manifestation as we journey beyond the veil of The Golden Age. You are always connected to Universal Mind, GOD, All That Is… It creates whatever you think about.

As water flows through the gentle streams and rivers into the spacious sea, so your consciousness joins the steady stream of mass awareness through the Universe. All mind is ONE mind, and as humanity's memory ignites the Flame of Realization that we are One in Spirit, the Cosmic Bridge is strengthened. Your thoughts hold a vibration and zoom out into the mass pool of thought, instantaneously creating a result from which you intended, for energy follows thought. Your words are very powerful and have the ability to shift another person's consciousness when you speak from your Heart to serve their highest good. This is why we ask you to go into silence, within the stillness of your heart, several times a day and be aware of your thoughts, feelings, and your spoken words. Your word is your wand and places your order with the Universe continually. In the coming era, your thoughts and words will be sent telepathically, and the results may manifest before your sentence is even complete. For this reason, Dear Beloveds, we ask that you practice the Power of Intent, for each and every thought affects ALL Beings on the planet. You are constantly connected to Universal Mind. As you CONSCIOUSLY select your thoughts and intentions, you reshape the fabric of the world...What you think and believe streams out into the Sea of Consciousness and supports others as they grow. So when sitting in moments of silence, send LOVE out into the Universe to ALL creatures great and small. Send love to all Beings, everywhere, for this will increase the frequency of the Earth and unite all souls throughout the Galaxies, strengthening the Planetary Grid and Interdimensional Bridge of Light. I AM Aurora.

Affirmation: I AM standing in my EMPOWERMENT now.

I AM a Divine Alchemist, the Majestic Master of my thoughts and words in each and every moment.

IMAGINATION

Your Imagination is the canvas through which you create your Reality.

Allow yourselves to bask in the childlike wonder and imagination of visualizing every area of your life exactly the way you wish it to be, Children of Light, for your IMAGINATION is the canvas through which you create your Reality.

Dear Ones, we ask that you not focus or dwell on what you do *not* wish to experience, but instead on *what you would like to attain,* and to move toward it confidently, as if you have already achieved it... Let your cup runneth over with beautiful dreams and ideals, and do not be dismayed by the reactions and responses of others, for through your steadfast faith, you shall manifest your desires and be a Guidepost to many. The Spark of God within you is your Imagination, your golden key. When you believe within your heart, with unwavering faith, with absolute KNOWINGNESS, then *ANYTHING* is possible...for *knowingness* is the step beyond *believing.* As you begin to see yourself as the magnificent, majestic soul that you are, empowered and fully capable of being all that you came here to be, you radiate the Light of Creator, strengthening the Crystalline Planetary Grid and claiming your birthright as Co-creator.

Hold fast to the enchantment within your hearts, to all that is lovely and true to you, for through your unwavering perseverance, all that you desire shall be yours by divine right. So Beloveds, permeate your consciousness with FAITH. Be still and know that you are God, a Divine Alchemist. I AM Aurora.

Affirmation: I AM basking in my Imagination, through which I create my reality.

I AM one with Divine Knowingness.

AWAKEN
TO THE CALL WITHIN

As you awaken to the call within, you join the Legions of Light.

We ask you to don your Radiant Swords of Light and join the unified efforts of the Air Fleet Command of the Most Radiant One, alongside the Beings of Light, to assist in this most vital assignment on Planet Earth. The *time is now* to activate within, to share your light, understanding, and teachings with the world at large. The entrance and expansion beyond the veil of The Golden Age will have a building or layering effect, and it will take some time for all of the upgraded earth energies to acclimate and settle in, for the Ascension of the planet is a gradual process and the earth will take time to integrate the new energies of Spirit and fully soar in the coming years ahead. As we have stated, this is a process, and things will not happen in the blink of an eye. So we ask you to stay the course beside us, and hold the field assisting Mother Earth through the assimilation of matrixes, layers, and petals of geometry as your beautiful planet journeys into the new Era of Terra, Planet Earth as a star.

Each and every one of you reading these pages have received the clarion call to answer the song within, to step forward and join the Legions of Light as we move most graciously into the ever-anticipated Age of Aquarius. Many have been called but have ignored their inner prompting. Some have gotten too distracted with everyday events of their three-dimensional lives and have chosen not to listen. Some have not turned toward the stillness of meditation to bask in the energies of divine knowingness, to feel the presence of the Great Teachings. We hold these souls in our hearts and await the day that they too may be awakened in the Light of Spirit. But for you today, we honor and applaud you, for you have answered the call within, and you have abided by the Laws of the Universe at this most urgent time on the planet. We ask that you radiate your magnificent light to all you meet, to tell your story of awakening to all who will listen, to joyfully speak to your friends, family, and acquaintances, for it is through these communications that others will begin to prepare and merge into this most vital planetary transition.

You vowed to come to Planet Earth at this time, to embrace the opportunity to be an Ambassador of Light, to set energetic templates and raise the frequency of all you meet, through your words, voice, creative talent, service, and song. For this, we honor you greatly. In infinite service, I AM Aurora.

Affirmation: I AM an Ambassador of Light.

I AM holding the field for Mother Earth's Ascension.

RETURN
TO
LOVE

The New Dimensional Reality.

Earth is beginning its return to LOVE. In this new 5th dimensional reality, nothing less than love can exist, for within the new domain of Terra resides the frequency of pristine purity.

Energy surrounds every living thing. As you begin to see these subtle fields, you KNOW there is a higher dimensionality to ALL living creation. We ask that you take particular care of nature and all of the elementals and creatures around you, for each living entity is connected to another. Every species on earth serves a purpose in the divine plan and reflects back to you, what you need to see.

You are a Conduit of higher light frequency. When you welcome the TRUTH of who you are, you activate dormant light codes within, igniting a deep core memory of Oneness and All That Is. As you share your light with others, you assist in the soul awakening of humanity, and the doorway is opened for the return to love in the new dimensional reality. The world that you are preparing to enter will exist on a level and frequency of Unity Consciousness, for as your Great Teacher Sananda has said… "Where you are, I AM."

You will begin to see these changes taking place over the next several years of your current earth calendar, and we ask that you follow and honor your inner gauge, for by doing so, all will unfold into the magical Heaven on Earth. The time is NOW for your beautiful planet to awaken and merge with higher Consciousness, the Consciousness of Christ. Many have asked what they can do to prepare for this upcoming rebirth as Earth crosses the veil and emerges on the other side of the planetary matrix. What we would like to say is, the very fact that you are reading these pages makes you a faithful member of the Allegiance of Light. There will be many who do not make this shift of consciousness and ascend with your planet, but for you it is to fill your bodies with LIGHT and hold this frequency wherever you go, for in doing so, you raise the frequency of those around you. Be the Beacons of Light that you are... The etheric Light Houses that you have created on your properties radiate the high vibrational velocity of YOU. BE in the Light, BREATHE in the energy of Spirit and FEEL our warm embrace in your heart, for we are always with you. We are the Beings of Light and Aurora, beside The Most Radiant One, in divine service and love always.

Affirmation: I AM a Conduit of higher light frequency.

I AM radiating LIGHT to all I meet.

MORE TRUTH
SHALL
SET YOU FREE

The King of Kings. Through His name, you shall be saved.

Modern day religion has been misconstrued and twisted at the hands of man for personal gain and control of the masses. For this reason, many of the earthborn race have been turned off by "religion" and the strict constraints placed therein. What we would like to tell you is that the Heart of Spirit was never meant to be manipulated and dissolved in such a horrific manner, for God is All Loving, All Knowing, All Accepting. God does not control, connive, and twist, manipulating out of fear. God does not threaten you and hover over you with an iron-clad weapon. For God is LOVE and God dwells in each and every one of your hearts, guiding and directing you always. In the days ahead, those people of inner authority who have misused their power through His sacred name will be brought to justice for their misdeeds and removed from their places of duty within the church, for there is no place for mind control or evil behavior in the higher realms of Spirit. This is not to say that ALL officials of the cross have been misrepresentative of His word. The masses know who these individuals are, many in the upper echelons of the majestic Cathedrals and Temples. In the days to come, hold the light in your heart, for all is unfolding as it should in the divine tapestry of the Universal Cathedrals of Light. We hold the Torch of Light for all to see the truth, for the truth shall set you free. I AM Aurora.

Affirmation: I AM LOVE.

I AM a vessel of Truth and Divine Wisdom.

VESSELS
OF LIGHT

Your bodies as your personal crafts.

Every moment you spend sending light and love to others, increases your soul's Illumination. Become a TRANSMITTER of higher dimensional energy.

Every time you connect with the LIGHT, you build a bridge between yourself and the higher dimensional plane of Spirit. Your physical vessels hold an immense amount of light and as you cross the energetic veil beyond The Golden Age, you will continue to build your Body of Light, for through this vessel you will travel. In the years ahead, your vessels will serve as your personal crafts, teleporting you to any geographical destination of your choice. Your vessel is capable of holding a huge amount of energy, for this is what builds and amps up your light body. Like the fuel for a car, your body will require LIGHT. So every day, in every way, fill your vessel with light. Simply state, "I AM flooding my body with White Light now". Radiate this energy to all you meet, for when you share your light with others, your vessel replenishes and GLOWS. As you continue to *recycle* this high velocity light energy, an immense frequency emanates from your heart. We would also ask you to spend time out of doors in the natural sunlight, and allow yourself to bask in the energy of the sky, for this too fills your body with light. In doing so, you hasten your acceleration process on a vaster level, becoming a Beacon of Light for all you meet. I AM Aurora.

Affirmation: I AM a Beacon of Light and Love.

I AM upgrading my energy matrixes now.

JOYFUL
INTENT

You are a DIVINE ALCHEMIST. The doorway is open… Step through and explore your highest vision.

You are a Magnificent Being born with a specific purpose, a customized role that no one else can fulfill. As you acknowledge the sacredness of your existence on the planet at this time, you open a portal of opportunity to be of service in a grand way.

What would you do if you could do anything, Dear Beloveds… Through the action of your heart, your destiny will be revealed, for each of you is here to fulfill a specific purpose on this plane and it involves a joyous heart and intent. Open your heart and mind, and ask to be guided to this beautiful understanding in the coming days and you will receive the appropriate downloads and insights to guide you. As my Brothers and Sisters of Light in the Sky Borne Division have taught through the violet flame teachings and decrees, I direct you to this knowledge of spiritual transformation. For through the violet flame, the heart center is cleansed and your soul is refreshed and replenished in the purity of Spirit. Open you heart to these teachings and you will be amazed by the transformation in every area of your life…you will serendipitously be placed in exact, direct synchronicity with your soul's spiritual mission. It is indeed an honor to be alive on the earth plane at this time in the history of the Galaxies, and your unique destiny is calling you like never before.

Perhaps there are some of you who sense you have fulfilled the majority of your spiritual contract and are slowing down your pace… For those, we would invite you to stay open to the realization that there is MORE TO COME! The time is now to open ever wider to the spark within and embrace the full emergence of Spirit. The following I AM affirmation will place you directly where you need to be in the Universal flow for your soul's infinite unfoldment… "I AM activating and living my divine blueprint now". As you state or chant this affirmation throughout the day, you will be proportionately centered with the proper celestial energies to place you in the right place at the right time. Yes, it is as simple as that. Ask and you shall receive, affirm and KNOW that all is in perfect order. I AM Aurora and I bring you these messages today.

Affirmation: I AM embracing the JOY in my heart now.

I AM activating and LIVING my divine blueprint now.

LOVE
TURNS THE KEY

As humanity's memory ignites the Flame of Realization that we are ONE in Spirit, the Cosmic Bridge is strengthened, for where you are, I AM.

When you act in the capacity of Love, you BROADCAST high velocity electromagnetic rays, healing hearts and transforming the vibration of the planet.

LOVE LOVE LOVE... The frequency of Love turns the key. If you could only know how much you are loved and admired in the higher celestial realms of Spirit you would never want for anything. For love is what shall lift the planet up to its rightful place in the Galaxies as Mother Earth transitions into a star. We shower you with energy from our heart centers and assist you in igniting and expanding your three-fold flames within, for the HEART is the conduit through which the I AM Presence communicates. When the day comes that we are united in Spirit, you will feel our warm embrace and your heart centers shall glow with the well-lit light of REMEMBRANCE that WE ARE ONE. It may be difficult for you at first to contain this astounding vibration, for it is beyond anything you have been capable of experiencing and sustaining thus far in your existence on this plane. We look forward to the day when we will be merged together in the Light of The Most Radiant One. We hold the candle of faith within our hearts for you as you ignite your flames of glory! I AM Aurora.

Affirmation: I AM fully embodying the waves of light that fan
the three-fold flame within.

I AM Broadcasting high frequency light now.

POWER POINTS
ON
THE PLANET

When you explore the multidimensional doorways that are open to you, you activate ancient cellular memories and a deeper remembrance of self emerges.

There are numerous power spots all over the world where crafts enter and exit through portals. Some of you have power points or vortexes on your personal properties where your Star Families of Light enter and exit from time to time, downloading and teaching you what is needed to know at different times throughout the day. Other power spots include areas in Sedona, Mt. Shasta, New Mexico, Tibet, Peru, Egypt, India, the Yucatan, Africa, Estes Park, Stonehenge, and the Midwest to name a few. As people frequent these areas they receive downloads and infusions of light which amplify their energy fields, upgrading and recalibrating their energetic matrixes to a level that is needed for their soul's evolution and catapult into their light bodies. Each soul will be drawn to the area that best suits their merkabic needs for upgrading and upliftment. We would ask that you allow yourself to travel to areas of inner prompting without second guessing yourselves so that you will progress in the manner your soul intended.

Many individuals that do healing and creative work have chosen to live in vortex areas of sacred vibration, as it enhances the energies of their work and communication with the higher dimensional Beings that accompany them. In addition, many Starseeds have been drawn to live on land that has been frequented by UFO's and that has housed crop circles, as this is another means of communication with their Star Families of Light. This is very important to those of you who are Starseeds that are currently fulfilling your missions, as you are accompanied by crafts at your place of domain or residence (whether you consciously see them or not), to continually support, heal, and guide you, especially in times of rest and sleep. Some of you have been prompted to live in the natural countryside or outskirts of town, as Nature is vital in your evolution, faithfully assisting you as you hold the frequency for the planet. In divine adoration, we are the Beings of Light and Aurora.

Affirmation: I AM grateful for my Star Family of Light that guides and protects me.

I AM holding the field of light for humanity.

THE
MAJESTIC ONES

Turn your eyes to the sky.

Through our channel comes the song, "I feel like an Eagle in the morning sun, I can fly close to heaven, I can touch the sun..." Such a beautiful display and celebration of this most majestic bird of flight. Many of you that are working spiritually behind the scenes are drawn to this regal creature, for you are ONE with the Spirit of the Eagle. Your eyes may wander to the sky, only to be guided to this precious soul, for the Eagle holds the Heart of the Great Spirit, the Divine Creator of All. We ask, do you not feel washed over with peace and emotion when you are graced with the presence of this revered feathered friend? The Eagle brings you messages from the world of Spirit, and the vision and courage to move forward on your path with strength and valor. Those of you that are Starseeds, Radiant Warriors, and Light Servers are kin to the Eagle, and whether you realize it or not, you have made the covenant to come to the planet at this time to bathe in the Light of Spirit, to lift your hearts to the sky, to commune with the beauty of nature, claiming and redeeming your power, and to radiate this divine knowingness of Creator. For you are Majestic Beings of Light in flight...like the Eagle... You have vowed to assist Mother Earth, in and through your service to humanity. You have heard the call within and recognized the familiar song in your hearts. So you take flight with the Eagle, side-by-side anchoring in the new energies of Heaven on Earth, as your beloved Terra transcends to her new station in the stars... I AM Aurora of Light, ever vigilant in my service to humanity.

Affirmation: I AM one with the Spirit of the Eagle.

I AM a faithful Servant of the Light.

NATURE
REPRISE

The Beauty of Nature cannot ever be fully captured in its divine magnificent splendor... It must be felt with the heart.

As humanity awakens to the realization that you are but GUESTS on this beautiful planet, a divine understanding is ignited in the hearts of man, for when mankind strives to live harmoniously and sustainably as ONE, humanity sets a template igniting and catapulting the planet into the new Age of Light.

Beloveds, we ask you once again to describe how you feel when you spend time in the splendor of nature...for nature rejuvenates and supports your frequency and energetic make-up. The leaves, trees, rocks, mountains, streams and oceans release high vibrational violet rays of light that both energize and calm the soul at the same time. The power of nature is immense, for it also centers your being and supports your intuitive faculties, bringing through important downloads, insights, creative breakthroughs, and spiritual directives in your life. As you awaken to your Interconnectedness with Nature and All That Is, you merge more fully with Universal Consciousness, creating a better world for all souls and creatures of the planet. So it goes without saying, it is imperative to spend time communing out of doors in all seasons, for through the beauty of nature, inner keys and filaments are ignited and activated, assisting you in your healing and movement forward on the New Earth, creating betterment for all.

Nature is a reflection of mankind and the Universal Mind's wisdom, intelligence, and action, so we would ask that you take the time to be a Steward of the Earth. Mother Earth is ALIVE and assesses every step you take on her sacred ground, gauging your level of commitment and willingness to be of service. You are on the trail to Higher Consciousness... As you open up to Mother Earth and communicate your INTENTION for being alive, your path is lit. So love, tend to, honor, cherish, commune, and replenish the glory that she has so graciously provided, as she has faithfully supported and held watch over you while you have journeyed through this plane. I AM Aurora.

Affirmation: I AM a joyful Steward of the Earth.

> I AM bestowing blessings on Mother Earth now.

SOUL PODS

Unity Consciousness & Children.

Love, nurture, and embrace those souls closest to you, for they have chosen to walk beside you as you journey and evolve on this plane.

Hold true to your vision of Love & Unity for all, Children of Light, for in the days ahead, your vision will be realized. Surround your most precious images in pink and white light and send them out into the Universe wrapped with joy from your heart, for you are the master creators, and as your Great Teacher Sanada has promised, as intended – so it shall be. We have made this promise to you and assist you in this intergalactic endeavor of love, peace, unity and equality for all. We ask that you infuse your desire with powerful emotion, as you back your intentions with love and the intent of Spirit.

We would especially ask that you embrace and nurture the precious children that have chosen to come in with you on this plane in your soul pods, for they too have chosen to make their entrance at this time, prewired and ready to assist in buffering the energies of those lesser ones and in bringing through information to assist the masses in the years ahead. These are the Indigos, Crystals and Rainbow Beings. These amazing souls are blessed with immense talent and their energetic matrixes have been preprogrammed spiritually. Many of these profound souls have chosen challenging lessons to assist in the expedition of their soul's evolution. Some have chosen abuse to overcome, Attention Deficit Disorder, Down's Syndrome, Autism, and other bodily limitations, but beneath their flesh surface exists an extremely advanced Being, a Living Master, with spiritual and technical information to share. To the dismay of your Galactic Brothers and Sisters of Light, the earthen society has placed some of these children in the corner, locked them away, or filled them with prescription drugs. What is needed for these advanced souls is "energy" medicine and love. So be patient. Love, honor and protect your blessed children of the Earth, including those that are not yours from birth, for they are Children of the Future and belong to us all. I AM Aurora.

Affirmation: I AM showering light on God's precious ones.

I AM an advocate for the Children of Light.

PRECIOUS
LINK

You are a precious link in the unified Global cause.

You are a Divine Being who volunteered to be on the planet at this time to assist in the mass awakening of humanity. Whether you have integrated this understanding or not, it is so, for there are many souls who requested to come here at this point in time and be a part of this Historic Galactic Celebration, but were denied. We again ask you to remember that each and every individual you encounter in your days on this plane, came here with the distinct intention of AWAKENING to the Light of Spirit and becoming One with God. Some have not yet interpreted the clarion call and this is not to be judged, for as we have spoken before, all souls have been granted the gift of free will and what they choose to do with their incarnation is their divine choice and destiny. Some souls on the planet have fallen through the cracks and engaged in travesties or evil acts. For these souls, they will exist in a lower dimensional reality and not join the earth in her Ascension off the 3-D plane at this time. These challenged souls will still be given the opportunity to evolve in the light and heal on a different dimensional platform, at which later time they may make the leap of Ascension to a higher state of being. Through loving service, I AM Aurora.

Affirmation: I AM a precious link in the unified
Global cause.

I AM a compassionate Being of Light
holding the field for humanity.

CITIES
OF LIGHT

Intergalactic Cities of Light...The way of the future.

There are Intergalactic Cities above you with Cosmic Beings existing on a different dimensional plane of supreme wisdom and intelligence. These cities in the sky are located directly above you and when you are vibrating at a higher velocity, you will be able to see our silver chariot cities with intergalactic buildings and architectural delights. We have chosen to be above you at this time to monitor your energies and evolution, and to provide you with necessary downloads needed in order to raise the planet's frequency and assist in ushering you more fully across the veil of energy into The Golden Age. There will be a time soon, in days ahead, when we will walk beside you and co-exist in peace, honor and love for ALL.

As the earth shifts into its new SPHERICAL reality, mankind opens the doorway to higher dimensionality, co-creating unity and harmony with all Beings throughout the Galaxies, as we joyfully celebrate an unprecedented, intergalactic co-existence throughout the Universe. As your faithful Servant of Light, I AM Aurora.

Affirmation: I AM utilizing my multidimensional spiritual capacities now.

I AM receiving Spirit-sanctioned downloads now.

STAY
THE COURSE

To be ALIVE on the planet at this time is to take responsibility for the immense DEPTH of your soul and to fully embrace the mission you are here to fulfill.

Do not lose sight of your missions, Beloveds, for as you cross the veil beyond The Golden Age, your energy is needed to hold the vibrational field of those around you, as humanity expands its merkabic range of motion. You are intricate pieces of the puzzle... Each of you came to the planet at this time to perform a particular task that only YOU can fulfill. As you honor your soul's unique spiritual path, you shine light on humanity, the Galaxy, the Universe. Trust in yourselves, for you are spectacular Temples of Living Light, Emissaries and Avatars of the new Era of Terra. Each of you has a distinct plan to fulfill, and without your unwavering dedication, the puzzle pieces will scatter. So we ask that you have FAITH, stay the course, forge ahead with grand fortitude, and beautifully step into your soul blueprints that patiently await you. Trust the insights you receive, and you shall expand the portal of cosmic knowledge, becoming Conduits of this high vibrational wisdom, bridging the way for many. Those of you reading these pages have already begun this process. Some of you (particularly those who are specialists in assisting other planets in Ascending) have been doing your work for years, and are at this time holding the field for others to do the same. You have gone in ahead and prepared the space, you have taken your positions in the battle of Light and dark, and you have held firm to the Light of God. Where there is profound Light, no darkness can exist and we have reached a level of Light on the planet that will sustain, support, and assist your beloved Mother Earth in her transition into a star. We salute you all with great honor and hold the Torch of Light for you, regardless of your level of advancement...for we are ONE. We shower you with blessings and love. I AM Aurora.

Affirmation: I AM holding the vibrational field for
humanity now!

I AM a faithful Carrier of Light!

LIFE MATES
IN THE GOLDEN AGE

Starseed Mates

There are those of you who have been faithful disciples on the path for decades now, and are still awaiting spiritual mates of a high enough vibrational caliber to reside with you on the New Earth, as you fulfill your soul missions on a deeper level and merge into the Age of Light. For you, we know it has not been easy as you have traveled the Path of Light on your own, but as The Most Radiant One has counseled, "Fear not, you are not alone"...for a tremendous amount of spiritual growth occurs when you are an individual entity of light. As we direct you to the word, "aloneness", we invite you to interpret it as "all-ONE-ness". Many of you that have vowed to walk this higher dimensional road have ended up traversing it alone, and we salute you for your courage, patience, and perseverance, as we know it has not been easy. Some of you, fully realizing that you have been in your own personal quickening, have determined that in order to experience the greatest amount of progress on your path, you must journey in a single fashion through various seasons of your life. We greatly honor you.

Relationships teach you much, however, some earthlings have become challenged and distracted off their course because they have lost sight of themselves through co-dependency and co-existence in partnership. Many couples are evolving at different rates and some individuals choose to stay stagnate and halt their growth for the other. The key is to "enhance" each others lives, give each other space to fulfill your own personal *individual* purpose, yet hold hands and soar beautifully into the future.

For those who have not partnered, we make the promise that your true divine conscious mates will appear on the horizon ahead, for they are of a pristinely high dimensional stature, many from other star systems. They are already beside you etherically and will present themselves in the time to come, so that you may walk hand in hand in the New Heaven on Earth. In love and service, I AM Aurora.

Affirmation: I AM easily traveling the Path of Light.

I AM meeting now my true divine spiritual Partner of Light!

SOUL
REMEMBRANCE

Remember the souls that have walked before you.

Love, appreciate, and cherish the kindred spirits that have left the earth before you, for they willingly chose to walk beside you as you have journeyed and evolved on this plane.

Many have asked why there are so many souls that have chosen to exit the earth plane before the Great Emergence of Light. For these souls, the reasons are vast. You may have recently noticed a particularly large number of young people leaving the planet. We will address those first. There are a large quantity of Indigo and Crystal children that have left your plane to assist in holding the energetic field on the other side, in preparation of the Golden Age Era, for there needs to be a fine balance of multidimensional energies woven into the divine blueprint of the Planetary Grid to assist the earth in shifting to its new orbital place. Release your heavy hearts, for these beautiful spirits have chosen to be of grand service, through soul agreement, long before they were birthed. Please know the work these beloveds do is Spirit sanctioned, for they are the Brave Warriors of Light. In the days to come, you will understand their message and mission on a large scale.

Additional younger souls who have departed have done so to crack open the hearts of those left behind, in order to cause an AWAKENING to occur, which may not have otherwise happened, so that their survivors may shift their energies, open their heart chakras, and be prepared to make their alignment into the light. Certain unexpected deaths have occurred in your celebrity arena as well. These souls have held a high frequency of light for the masses and have contracted at this time to assist in holding the field on the other side as well, weaving together the divine tapestry of the Crystalline Galactic Grid.

Many of you have been heartbroken about your beloved pets and four-leggeds that have departed, some with undue cause. These precious souls, many who were owned by higher dimensional earthlings, Light Servers and Starseeds have made their transition. We will explain that these four-legged beings have been apprenticed well under their earthly masters to hold the frequency of light and the vibrational frequency of the New Earth. These faithful servants have been called to cross the veil and go in ahead, to serve in the frontline, connecting their energetic matrixes with their earthly owners, forming a Celestial Grid or webbing, that will assist greatly in raising the planet to its divine location in the galaxy. Imagine your favorite pets positioned in a huge horizontal frontline, with their galactic shields of light radiating, your faithful Warriors of Light, assisting in this most vital process. We tell you this to warm your hearts, to let you know you are still very closely connected, always ONE in Spirit. Animals understand physical death, unlike many humans. They realize they are still very much alive and that they simply exist in a different dimensional state of being. What a joyful celebration it will be when you are reunited in the coming days. For now, we ask you to embrace those heartfelt souls that are embodied around you, those dear ones in your soul pod, for you have traveled many lifetimes to be together at this particular point on the planet, to walk hand-in-hand in the Light of Spirit as Mother Earth journeys beyond the veil into The Golden Age. We bless you always. I AM Aurora.

Affirmation: I AM grateful for my shared journey with my Earth family.

I AM eternally blessed in my relationships with my animal family, domestic and wild.

INTERGALACTIC
COMMUNICATION

Cosmic Communication…We are with you.

Look into the night sky and you shall see us. When you open up to our communication and clarity, we are there. We may appear as a twinkling light, a white light that glistens and disappears. We may appear as a large sphere that glides quickly across the sky, or in our Christed Chariots coming in close. We have also been known to move around in a "sprinkling" affect, or appear as ORBS. We would like to make your acquaintance and let you know we are here on a Christed Mission, and have always been. The thinning layers of recent times have allowed us to make communication with you more clearly. This opening has made it easier for us than in the past. There will be days in the future when you may hear tapping, clicks, or as you say, morse code, in one of your ears. You may also experience substantial ringing, or a marked humming that can be quite prevalent. These are all ways that we tell you we are present and would like to make contact. So we would ask at that time, that you stop what you are doing, sit down in stillness, and open up to our loving insight and communication. This will be channeled knowledge that flows easily and effortlessly through you. Some of you have already experienced this gift and are assisting humanity on a large scale with the information you have transcribed. Some have put their messages to mankind through writing, song, film, or other forms of creative expression and talent to reach the masses. We salute you all. We are entering the glory days and the glory days will be divine, for you are exalted in your dedication and service to the planet. I AM Aurora.

Affirmation: I AM seeing and communicating clearly with my Star Family of Light now.

I AM utilizing my multidimensional gifts to assist humanity now.

SOUL AGREEMENTS
TO AWAKEN

Every Being on the earth plane came here at this time to Awaken and find FREEDOM in the Light.

Dear Ones, many of you have had questions about parents, siblings, or older generational family members in your soul group who do not appear to be open to understanding the frequency of light and emergence into the higher planes of reality. Again, these beloveds have free will and will make their choice in due time in accordance with their soul's prompting and desire. It is again important to remember that each soul, upon divine timing, ignites memories and codes within, activating the teachings they need to hasten growth, and propel them forward on this plane. As we have previously stated through our channel, many have made the heartfelt agreements to awaken closer to the eve of the entrance into the New Age of Light, beyond the veil, as the New Earth assimilates and evolves into her new galactic rotation in the stars. There will be those of you who will serve as Gatekeepers, if you will. As the Gatekeepers and Light Servers, you will cross the veil first with Mother Earth, then journey back and forth through the dimensional doorway, bridging the gap to assist those who have chosen to be in a *holding pattern*, so to speak. Those souls, while in their holding patterns, will make their decision as to whether or not they choose to make their leap in Consciousness and awaken. Some of the events may be heartfelt, but necessary for their advancement and evolution into the light, for every soul on the planet came here with the initial intention of awakening and evolving into a Higher Dimensional Being. We open our hearts and stand free of judgment, holding the field for these beloved souls to make their decision, for there will be many who choose to ignite their ancient memory of self on the cusp of this celebrated event. For those who do not, we bathe them in love and light, judgment free, allowing them to partake in their universal gift of free will. We faithfully stand by your side, ever vigilant, as your Brothers and Sisters of Light. I AM Aurora.

Affirmation: I AM a Conduit of Light, holding the field for those who wish to awaken.

I AM a faithful Gatekeeper, assisting others in their Ascension process.

INTERGALACTIC
HEALING CHAMBERS

Healing Chambers in the New Era of Terra.

Dear Ones, we invite you to enter our Light Synthesis Healing Chambers at night, when you have laid down to rest, for we assist you in your healing and rejuvenation process. For those of you that are guided, we ask that you call upon the Christed Cosmic Healing Chamber of Light to assist you in upgrading your light quotient, heal your physical distress, and assist in your light body recalibration process. For through this portal you will be healed. In future times, there will be light-filled healing chambers, tangibly located throughout the Cities of Light as you emerge on the other side of The Golden Age and continue to assimilate the powerful energies of the New Earth. It will take some time to hold the monumental amount of light that will be available on the planet and these chambers are a way to fully integrate and maintain these new intergalactic frequencies. In infinite devotion, I AM Aurora.

Affirmation: I AM infused with the Golden Liquid Light of
the Christed Cosmic Healing Chamber now.

I AM upgrading my light quotient now.

LEGIONS OF LIGHT

You are being prompted to your mission through all your days... Tap into the energy of your soul's blueprint and remember the gifts you are here to share with the world.

You are here to assist in the transcendent mass awakening of the planet. To REMEMBER your grand and splendid purpose. Each of you came to the Earth at this time to perform a particular task, to share your unique experiences and abilities, to face your challenges, and to bring light...to help create and strengthen the Bridge of Light. We ask that you call upon the sword of Archangel Michael and step bravely into your missions, for the masses need you. Every single one of you reading these words has a specific duty and allegiance in the planetary shift as Mother Earth makes her splendid alignment in the stars. Everything that you have experienced in your life has prepared you for your soul's purpose and evolution into the Light of Spirit. If you are not clear what it is that you are to do, simply open up and state, "I AM ready and willing to fulfill my divine blueprint now"! In the following days, you will be guided through synchronicities, downloads and insights as to what steps to take. Ignite the ancient keys within and know that you are guided. Realize the task you are here to perform at this time of great change on the planet. As you do so, you enrich the lives of every Being you meet. Trust the process, Dear Beloveds, for doubt erases intuition and builds an iron-clad fortress around your consciousness. So we ask that you have faith… TRUST, BELIEVE and KNOW that you are divinely guided in every way. I AM Aurora.

Affirmation: I AM divinely guided in each and every moment.

I AM basking in the energy of KNOWINGNESS now.

EMERGENCE
OF LIGHT

Light emerging beyond the veil.

Structure as it is known to Man is no longer tangible. Humanity must turn inward and discover the greater dimensional reality of Self in order to evolve and advance beyond the veil of the New Earth and all that it offers in this unprecedented time on the planet. Structure is changing and can no longer be determined solely by scientific methods and studies. Earth is inundated with infinite petals, diagrams, and portals of sacred geometry, language of light, and spiritual orbs that beautifully shower the plane, unceasingly, at tremendous speed. It is time to merge with this divine intelligence, to bask in the knowingness that you are a Multidimensional Being, capable of all that you desire. As Mother Earth shifts into her new SPHERICAL Reality, mankind opens the doorway to higher dimensionality, co-creating unity and harmony for all. As your Messenger of Light, I AM Aurora.

Affirmation: I AM embracing the uniqueness of All Beings.

I AM joining together in a unified Global cause, co-creating unity, peace, and harmony for ALL.

JOYOUS
REUNION

We hold you in our hearts.

Through the Air Fleet Command of The Most Radiant One, Sananda, we serve you... The joy in our hearts is immense, for you have stepped forward and answered the clarion call within. We surround you with many celestial crafts in the sky, too numerous to count, fine tuning and upgrading your energies. We patrol your planet, faithfully following our mission to assist the Earth in its entrance into the New Age of Light. We appear to you and communicate with you through our heart centers, always guiding and assisting you. We look forward to the day when we are able to fully decloak our silver chariots in the sky so that ALL will know our presence of Spirit, when we shall walk hand-in-hand as Brothers and Sisters of Light, building and expanding our Cities of Light in the most anticipated Heaven on Earth. We hold you in our hearts always. Through infinite service and love, I AM Aurora.

Affirmation: I AM activating the codes of consciousness stored within my Beingness now.

I AM a Temple of Living Light, multidimensional and fully awakened.

MESSAGE
FROM
AURORA

Message from Aurora:

As Aurora of Light, I come to bring you messages of PEACE,
FAITH & LOVE. I work primarily from the 9th and 11th
dimensions, at the right hand of The Most Radiant One,
assisting all who wish to heal, transmute and ascend. From
our vantage point, we see the humans struggling to attain the
light of consciousness, negating their circumstances through self
sabotage and fear. Have faith Children of Light, for it is your
Divine Destiny to walk hand-in-hand in the Light of Spirit,
where ALL things are possible, as you most joyfully create the
much anticipated and long-awaited Heaven on Earth as your
beautiful planet evolves beyond the veil of The Golden Age.

I AM Aurora and I AM honored to serve you and your most
beloved planet. I have guided many through their journeys into
the light and am a specialist in the field. I have manned the
Starship of your Great Teacher Sananda, The Most Radiant
One, and continue to stand by his side as he assists many souls
and races in their healing, awakening, and transmutational
process. We ask that you join hands with your Brothers and
Sisters of Light as your beautiful planet makes its leap into
the cosmic circle of the stars, to join the other Star Nations
and work hand-in-hand in creating a most majestic Heaven on

Earth. We ask that you bless Mother Earth for the role she has so generously played throughout your incarnation on her plane, for she has faithfully supported and nurtured you, as you have evolved through your personal dramas on the learning plane. Your linear existence is but a brief blink in the grand scheme of the Cosmos. We ask now that humanity rise to the occasion, that you give thanks, bless, and love her magnificent essence for so faithfully holding the field for you in your long-awaited awakening and journey into the Union of Stars. We rejoice and embrace all the members on Earth who have chosen to ride the wave of consciousness and join your Great Teacher Sananda in and through His name as you so diligently move into the Age of Aquarius, where there is peace, harmony, and love for ALL Beings and all Planetary Nations. We unite with you in the stars and salute you for remembering your role in this grand celebration into the LIGHT. I AM Aurora, in and through our beloved channel, Gia.

ABOUT
THE AUTHOR

Gia Govinda Marie is an intuitive healer, teacher, and channel, who lives in the Midwest with her beautiful daughter, Camille, and her beloved animals and forest creatures on their enchanted woodland acreage. As a noted leader in her field, Gia's private healing arts practice encompasses Reiki, Intuitive Energy Medicine, Spiritual Counseling, Meditation, and communing with Nature Spirits, Angels, and the Beings of Light. Gia has studied metaphysics for over 20 years and dedicates her life to raising the frequency of the planet and assisting others in their healing and Conscious Awakening process. She travels the country speaking and teaching, in an effort to raise awareness universally, and assist all who wish to live their light, heal, and AWAKEN, as Earth evolves *beyond the veil* of The Golden Age.

OTHER BOOKS
BY
GIA GOVINDA MARIE

"Bejeweled Heart, Awakening the Light Within"

A Collection of Powerful Affirmations & Writings
To Assist Humanity's Awakening
Into The Golden Age of Light

ORBS

Numerous Orbs on the lawn out in front of the house.

ORBS

Diamond-shaped Orbs around me on the land.

ORBS

Diamond-shaped Orb over my third eye and all around me.

HONOR
THOSE BEINGS
THAT HAVE WALKED BEFORE US

My beloved dog THORIN who crossed the veil on May 24, 2011.
He now walks beside me as a Guide.

SEE
THE SPARK OF GOD
IN ALL LIVING CREATURES

Me feeding "Lucky" the baby squirrel who
was blown out of his nest in a storm.

PRECIOUS
SOULS

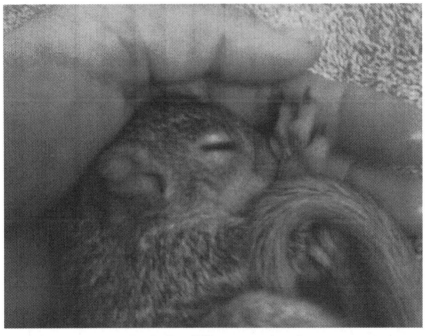

"Lucky" cuddling in my hand.

NATURE'S
CREATURES & BOUNTY
HAVE MESSAGES FOR US

All of Nature's creatures and bounty, even the
smallest of rose petals, have a message for us.
Tree frog housing in a rose bud outside the front door.

THE
MAJESTIC ONES

Golden Eagle, Creator's *Messenger of Light*
~Original artwork by my mom, Jena Brayton Hausknecht~

CHERISH
THOSE SOULS
THAT WALK BESIDE YOU

My daughter Camille and I.

BLESS
OUR BELOVED
ANIMALS

Animals are very intuitive and carry the frequency of LIGHT.
Gandalf at Thorin's grave on the anniversary of his crossing.

GO
INTO
STILLNESS

Meditation time at one of my favorite vortexes in Sedona.

"I salute
the light within your eyes
where the whole universe dwells.
For when you are at that center within you,
and I am at that place within me,
we shall be one".

~ Chief Crazy Horse ~
Oglala Sioux
1840-1877

GLOSSARY

Angels

Very loving, higher dimensional Etheric Beings, also known as Messengers of God, who are here to protect, guide, and watch over the souls in embodiment on Earth.

Akashic Records

High velocity etherical imprint that chronicles the memory of everything that has ever occurred, in or out of embodiment, through all space and time. Every thought, feeling, and impression is contained in this ethereal library and can be accessed through the development of psychic sight, or inner vision. The Akashic Records contain the entire history of every soul through the dawn of Creation, thus connecting us to one other.

Ascension

The process of planet earth raising its dimensional frequency to a high enough vibrational state to be transformed into a star.

Ascended Masters

Beings who have walked the earth before, who have fulfilled their divine plan, mastered Self, and fully realized the I AM Presence of God within. They are ascended in the higher realms with the purpose of guiding and teaching humanity. (Examples: Jesus, Buddha, St. Germain, Kwan Yin, El Morya, Kuthumi, Apollo, Metatron, Melchizedek, Moses, Ashtar, Mother Mary to name just a few).

Aura

The electromagnetic energetic field that surrounds an individual, Being, or object.

Beings

Light Beings, included but not limited to, Angels, Ascended Masters, Elementals, Nature Spirits, and other Cosmic Guides from various galaxies and star systems.

Bridge of Light

The ethereal bridge between the physical realm and higher light consciousness to the spiritual realms and beyond.

Buddha Nature

The innate wisdom of Buddha which is genetically housed in each and every one of us, waiting to be uncovered...at which point we are gifted with deeper wisdom, knowledge, peace, serenity, and compassion for all.

Cellular Memory

The cellular structure and complete memory blueprint within your genetic makeup that contains the database for ALL of your experiences, both positive and negative, through each and every lifetime, through all space and time. Every experience that has ever happened to you is stored in these cells. So, although you are incarnated on the earth plane in THIS lifetime, your cellular memory is *susceptible to*, and may be *triggered by*, events you currently experience, due to the memory and ancient knowledge contained therein. Once you are aware of this profound realization, you more easily integrate the understanding of Self, and soar on your spiritual path.

Chakras

Energetic vortexes in the etheric body based on Eastern Philosophy. There are many chakras throughout the entire system, with the focus being on the 7 main chakras from root to crown. The chakras correlate with the 7 colors and 7 notes on the musical scale. It is important to keep the chakras open and spinning beautifully, to allow for the proper circulation of energy (chi/ki/prana) to flow through the physical body, allowing one to maintain ideal health.

Children of Light

Those human beings that seek the Light and are being lovingly guided on their paths by Celestial Beings and other Cosmic Guides.

Christ Consciousness

The I AM Presence that dwells in each and every one of us, which awakens more fully upon the search for Light and Truth.

Christed Cosmic White Light

The highest frequency of Light available to the evolution of humanity, from the God Source and higher spiritual realms.

Christed ET's

Beautiful, higher dimensional Star People that work in the Light beside The Most Radiant One to assist humanity and Planet Earth in its Ascension and transition into a star, carrying out God's plan for the Universe where there is peace, love, and harmony for all.

Cosmic Angels & Beings

Advanced Beings from other galaxies, universes, and star systems that are here to help the human race awaken and evolve spiritually.

Divine Blueprint

Your own divine genetic library, spiritual web or map, that contains the charts of your ultimate spiritual mission that you contracted to fulfill on the earth plane in your higher dimensional state of being, where you create fulfillment, abundance, love, and service to humanity. Your Divine Blueprint holds information from your Guides, Angels, Ascended Masters & Teachers, Elementals, and the God Source.

Etheric

Higher dimensional space beyond the earth's atmosphere. Celestial realm.

Elementals

Nature Spirits and other Beings living in the natural realms of Spirit.

Frequency

The rate at which atoms and subparticles vibrate. Vibrating in your highest frequency brings you closer to God and raises the consciousness of the planet.

Golden Age of Light

The coming Age of Light where Mother Earth celebrates a higher level of Unity Consciousness, where all Beings on Earth and throughout the galaxies experience peace, love, and harmony for ALL.

Golden Liquid Light

Christed Cosmic Healing Light which flows down from the higher dimensional atmosphere, to all who request this profound healing energy.

Great White Brotherhood

The Spiritual & Celestial Order of Cosmic Beings, Angels, and Ascended Masters united together for the highest purpose of God on Earth.

Gridwork

The unconscious act by Light Servers and Starseeds of setting energetic templates wherever they go. These templates assist the earth in anchoring in higher light frequencies, which ultimately assist in the Ascension of the planet.

Higher Self

The I AM Presence, or Spark of God within.

Jewel of the Heart

The multifaceted Christ Consciousness center within the Secret Chamber of your Heart that houses the codes and keys to higher consciousness and your multidimensional self, which is activated upon spiritual awakening.

Keeper of the Flame

Those that have taken the vow to hold the violet flame of spiritual knowledge and transmutation within their hearts and utilize its energy to transform their lives, and grow spiritually.

Light Body

Your ethereal body in its perfected, superconscious state of being, which allows interdimensional communication and teleportation to other dimensional realities and spaces in time.

Light Servers

Incarnated souls that are awakening on the earth plane, working in the Light to carry out God's plan for the planet and universe.

Multidimensional

Relating to or having several spatial existences in different planes of energy.

Mutational Symptoms

Transitory physical symptoms that occur in your body as you raise your frequency and shift more fully into your higher dimensional state of being.

Nature Spirits

Fairy and Elfin Kingdom, also known as Elementals and Nature Spirit Realm.

Orbs

Emanations of higher dimensional Spiritual Beings, presenting in the form of sacred geometric shapes or symbols, which appear to be shimmering and floating, signifying the presence of Celestial Cosmic Beings, communicating and watching over you.

Orbs ~ Diamond-shaped

God is present. Sacred place. Higher dimensional work and communication with Celestial Cosmic Beings & Christed ET's.

Planetary Crystalline Grid

Also known as Crystalline Grid, Planetary Grid, Christ Consciousness Grid, Grid of Light. This elaborate holographic higher dimensional matrix of light is linked to all of the major portals, vortexes, power points, crystals, and cosmic doorways which connect planet earth to the higher dimensional spiritual realms, galaxies, and universes, ultimately creating an Intergalactic Bridge of Light, which assists humanity and all Beings in their healing, transformation, and transcendence into the new Age of Light, where there is peace, love and unity for all.

Sananda

Another name for Jesus, The Most Radiant One. He is the grand exemplar of each soul's Higher Christ Self or I AM Presence. Sananda purifies the cathedrals and temples, removing manmade dogma, doctrines and manipulation of the sacred book, which has corrupted the purity of His teachings.

Secret Chamber of the Heart

The intimate sacred space, or spiritual treasure box within the heart where Heaven and Earth reside, and from where all creation emerges. The Secret Chamber houses the Three-fold Flame of God.

Starseeds

Evolved souls from other planets, galaxies, and star systems that have vowed to come to Planet Earth and assist the earthlings in their healing and conscious awakening process. These cosmic souls are in human embodiment, however, their galactic genes contain a "wake-up call" coding, which enables them to activate at a predetermined time in their incarnation to assist humanity's transformation and entrance into The Golden Age, where there is peace, love and harmony for ALL.

Teleportation

The method of being transported across distance and space instantly, in a higher dimensional state of energy, using thought form and light.

Templates

Energetic matrixes set in the earth which allow higher vibrational frequency from solar flares, astrological alignments or other cosmic events to enter the planet, assisting Mother Earth in her Ascension process.

Terra

Another name for Planet Earth, subsequent to her transition into a star.

The Most Radiant One

Master Jesus, also known as Sananda throughout the higher dimensional realms. He is a member of The Great White Brotherhood and mans the Sky Borne Fleet overseeing the Great Shift as Mother Earth ascends and transitions into a star.

Third Eye

Center of psychic vision, or psychic eye, located in the center of the forehead between the eyebrows. The third eye is part of the chakra system and can be activated by meditation and communing with God, your Buddha Nature, All That Is.

Three-fold Flame

The Divine Spark within, residing in the Secret Chamber of the Heart. The three flames which are blue, yellow, and pink represent the heavenly Trinity, expressing the energies of Father, Son and Holy Spirit. This flame is the essence of God, your Buddha Nature, All That Is.

Vibrational Frequency

The velocity at which atoms and subparticles vibrate in an individual or entity. The higher the vibrational frequency, the closer one is to the Light, God, their Buddha Nature, and All That Is.

Violet Flame

The violet flame of spiritual transmutation, which helps an individual transform all areas of their life, and awaken spiritually. Ascended Master St. Germain assists humanity in the teachings and understandings of the violet flame.

Vortex

Powerful entrance and exit portals of the energetic electromagnetic grid system, wherein high vibrational spiritual energies flow back and forth, beyond the earth, space and time.